Pete's Wicked Book
by Pete Takeda
http://members.aol.com/ptakeda1

Cover photo by Greg Epperson
www.gregepperson.com

MIKE TEA

Steve,

I hope you enjoy reading this as much as I enjoyed researching it... Thanks,

Climbing Magazine
0326 Highway 133, Suite 190
Carbondale, CO 81623
climbing@climbing.com

First Printing 2000

ISBN 1-893682-05-6

Printed in the United States of America

10 9 8 7 6 5 4 3 2 1

Pete's Wicked Start

In 1834 R.H. Dana signed on as a sailor and shipped out of Boston on the brig Pilgrim, bound for the then wild coast of California. During his two-year voyage around Cape Horn, up the California coast and back to Boston, Dana suffered mightily. An abusive captain worked him seven days a week. Food was in lean and wormy supply. Storms threatened to capsize the small vessel, while weeks of calm drove the crew mad.

Dana persevered by dwelling on one thought: someday he would return to friends, family, and the comforts of home.

But as the voyage drew to a close and the ship pulled back into Boston harbor, Dana suddenly found himself "in a state of indifference, for which I could by no means account." For Dana, the toil and danger of ship life, however hateful at the time, was real living. The prospect of easy land life bored him.

As climbers we face the same conundrum as Dana. We amp up for a wall, but as soon as we sink that first nut we wish we were back on the ground. Paradoxically, the instant we top out, we longingly recall the good old days of the wall.

While we can all live adventure and suffer the same, few of us can articulate its thrills and lamentations. Writing, it seems, is more difficult than leading A5.

Pete Takeda is of the rare breed who can climb and put his thoughts on paper. His prose captures the raw matter of climbing. In particular he can look at what it is that drives us to climb, and how climbing causes everything else in our lives to conform to its mold, right or wrong. Takeda, like Dana — who went on to pen the seafaring classic *Two Years Before the Mast* — is honest with the reader.

In 1990 I landed at *Climbing* magazine, where, in 1992, a manuscript plunked on my desk. It was a gritty big-wall account, full of Yosemite despondency, gin, and horror, of an early ascent of El Cap's *Aurora,* a big, hard wall with a reputation. Though the article was from an unknown writer, its lucid imagery burst from the page like white light. The author had the unusual gift of speaking from the gut.

The editors debated about one second then accepted Pete Takeda's first article, *Up against the Wall,* which you find reprinted in this book. That article kick started Takeda's writing career here at *Climbing.* Soon Takeda was writing a regular column and features and his name smacked familiar with the climbing populace.

Since then Pete has become a good friend and climbing partner. Together, we've shot the late-night breeze, and stalked new routes in Colorado and the Canyonlands. Outside Grand Junction, Pete found a cirque of unholy towers with rock so poor a carabiner could pry out a 12-inch bolt and where you could knock over entire formations with a bulldozer. We did three routes there before regaining our senses.

After six years I thought those climbs were behind me. Then for this book I got to re-read Pete's "The Good Earth," his account of the grand old Grand Junction tower-climbing days. Pete's article caused those memories to come flooding back. In particular I recalled topping out on the "Turkey Neck" formation and being stung by a swarm of flying ants that lived there. Now, sitting at this desk, belly full of food and my feet resting on carpet, I find myself in a state of indifference, for which I can by no means account. Thanks, Pete.

Duane Raleigh
Publisher and Editor in Chief

The Journey

It is 9 p.m. on Sunday, August 22, 1999. In three days I will get on a plane and fly to New Delhi with Dave Sheldon. We are going climbing in the Indian Himalaya.

It is fitting that on the eve of my departure I struggle to finish a piece of writing. That's been a my theme — the constant opposition of climbing and vocation. The line between an act and its portrayal often blurs or overlaps, sometimes robbing one or the other of vitality. That is my greatest challenge, to practice both climbing and writing as freely, honestly, and independently as possible.

I have been sorting out these things for a long time. I first climbed rock more than 19 years ago, when my friends and I played connect-the-dots on rough-hewn boulders at an abandoned quarry. I was the weakest and most timid of the dozen who started climbing that spring. It is ironic that today, I am one of the original few who still climbs.

What motivates me? Motives are a great puzzle. They are at the core of human endeavor. Perhaps in plumbing the depths of the mystery we surrender to its deeper embrace. Or do the rigors of climbing lead us to touch something pure and unadulterated? Such elemental questions are dreadfully vast. I gave up trying to contrive a definitive answer years ago. Despite attempted absences, I have always come back to climbing. I guess that is answer enough.

What follows is a collection of tales written as truthfully as possible. Some leave a sick feeling in my gut. I worry about how they will be taken, especially by the impressionable. In many instances my trail might have diverged into tragedy. My road has been perilous and no amount of sentimentality would drive me to re-live any of it. I have always yearned to know things as they are, to experience life, to understand people. From childhood I have always held a great distrust on how life is portrayed. I felt that real experience was the best teacher. This outlook is a curse and a blessing. Some of us learn the hard way — others just know.

I did my first published writing in college. I was a staff writer for the University News at Boise State University. Working for the school paper gave me a few college credits and a captive audience. When I quit college, I quit writing. It was years later, in 1990, that I rang up *Climbing* magazine from a Yosemite pay phone. I was peeved by the negative press Yosemite was receiving in the magazine. I reached then managing editor Mike Benge (now editor). He listened to me piss and moan for several minutes. Then he said, "Well, if you think there's anything worth telling, let's see it." That's the best thing any aspirant writer could hear. I finished a new-route report on Yosemite. It was published shortly thereafter. A year later I wrote a feature called "Up Against the Wall." The article (included in this book), with standard-setting photography by Greg Epperson, was a cover story. From then on, I wrote regularly for *Climbing*.

I have tried to quit both writing as well as climbing, fearing the hold both have on me. You come to understand the power of things when you strive against them. Sometimes I hate writing. I've spent days in front of a blank computer screen waiting for an idea. I've sat at a desk next to my bed wondering where I'll get the rent money. Given these realities, being a "writer" soon suffocates whatever romance one might associate with the act. I climb and I write. They are part of who I am.

— *Pete Takeda*

Beginnings
The formative years

"A man has to embrace fate — or at least accept it." The words ran through my mind as we rigged the next rappel. It was snowing lightly and Dave Sheldon and I were retreating from our highpoint on the unclimbed East Face of the Sharksfin on Meru, in India's great Himalaya.

The headache — the first sign of cerebral edema — that had plagued me for the last two days was gone. Funny what a few hundred feet of descent can do.

Dave and I had left food and gear cached three rappels above us. We'd already spent months, spread out over two attempts in as may years trying to climb this prize.

"A man has to embrace fate ..." I don't know where the words came from. I might have read them in a book, or my father might have told them to me years ago when I was too young to grasp what lay beyond the comfort of home.

As I started down the rope I didn't realize that this would be our last attempt on Meru, at least for this year. Even in retreat I vowed to try again. It has always been that way for me. I've tried, succeeded, failed, walked away but never quit. I glanced up the fact to our high point and looked beyond failure.

I was born in Spokane, Washington, but before I was old enough to remember, my parents relocated the family, including an older brother, to a tiny white house on Deacon Avenue in Moscow, Idaho, where my father taught math at the University of Idaho.

My father, Dr. Yozo Takeda, was born in the backwater village of Tanabu in northern Japan, during an era of dramatic social change. Japan had lost World War II, and the country was poverty stricken. The old order had fallen in the ashes of Hiroshima and Nagasaki. My father was orphaned at seven: his father died of a heart attach and his mother from childbirth complications.

Growing up alone in a society that nurtures conformity and exacts obedience, my father often did the unthinkable. "In middle school," he says, "I was class leader. One of my classmates was being beaten in front of the class by a teacher. As class leader I felt responsible to protect my underlings."

I stood up and said 'You better stop beating him. If you want to beat someone you can beat me, but remember what you do because when I grow up I will come back and beat you!" The teacher left the room aghast.

Four years after World War II ended my father, whose best future was shining shoes for hotel guests, left Japan and sought a brighter future in America.

He met my mother, Nobuko Konishi in 1959. They were both attending school in Columbia, Missouri. He was studying mathematics, she was studying statistics. My mother was the daughter of a prominent Tokyo doctor who had come to America under the auspices of learning to play the piano. She met my father, fell in love, and several years later they were married. My father's social status, an orphaned son who had fled the country, produced an unavoidable schism. The maverick immigrant professor had taken my mother from both her tradition-bound parents and from the country they'd hoped she'd return to. The rift was never mended even after my mother's death.

One of my first vivid memories was fear. I was three years old, wandering down the sidewalk from our clapboard house. It was a gray day. The trees were stark and bare. The sharp, fertile smell of autumn laced the air. Tractors plowed the land, which lay in dark brown anticipation beyond a fence line. I'd never seen these rending, tread-clanking beasts, and was paralyzed by the metallic violence. My mother came along in a few minutes and rescued me, although, as is the case with most fears, I never really had anything to worry about.

Two years later, we moved to Boise, Idaho. Boise, the state capital, was a quiet and conservative town. The white-flight boom of the 1980s, when droves of Californians began flooding other Western states, had yet to hit. Boise had a small-town feel mingled with a blend of agrarian values and the liberal hipness of the Pacific Northwest.

1970. Kent State, the era of Nixon, and the slow decay of the America my father had sought. I passed time, blissfully unaware of most of the chaos of the decade. My parents worked, my mother at the Public Library and my father at Boise State College. My brother and I built plastic models, drew, painted, and read voraciously. Keith, a youth of brilliant mind and rampant curiosity, maintained a 4.0 grade point average from the 6th grade on. He parleyed a sharp intellect into a degree in math from Yale, and went on to earn a law degree from the University of Michigan. Today, he lives in New York City, working for a large law firm. I've always been proud of Keith — his achievements gave me a sense of legitimacy during my times of gravest self-doubt.

Midway through the 1970s, we moved to a housing development on a bench east of town. Below our neighborhood the shelf dropped off steeply to the swift currents and bottomland of the Boise River. Several miles upstream was a canyon lined with 60-foot black basalt cliffs. Beyond the river to the south and west lay flat, open sage country. Our red-brick house marked the transition between suburb and scrub-brush foothills. The hills were littered with jagged brown and red boulders, ranging from flat, three-foot-high plaques to large chunks jutting at odd angles. Our front yard was a jumbled mass of lichen-spotted sandstone — not high enough to climb, but wild and erratic enough to infect a young mind with an appreciation of natural chaos.

The low, rolling expanses behind the house rose roughly north to an abrupt plateau — Table Rock. Sandstone cliffs up to 30-feet high ringed this long, squat formation. The western terminus was lined with freshly cleaved planes of an old quarry. The quarried rubble was haphazardly stacked like a fallen-down ziggurat. The larger, 15- to 30-foot-high blocks lay among the rubble like Stonehenge gone askew.

Because of our hilltop location, I was able to enjoy trolling through the hills, turning over rocks, and scrambling around. In junior high my buddy, Paul Miller, and I would walk home from school, balancing around on the railroad tracks that cut through two miles of subdivision, back road, and golf course. The railroad paralleled the river, where we soon found a year-round jungle playground. There was swampy wading, tall trees, and dense undergrowth. As little delinquents, we'd build fires and drink the cheap wine we'd get older guys to buy. Sometimes Paul and I would fish, climb trees, and chew tobacco until we were sick.

Something went seriously wrong with us by the end of our junior-high years. Maybe it was rebellion against the autocracy of our parents. Maybe we were guinea pigs of the failed social experiment called the 1960s. Maybe I had to find my own way because my parents were lost between cultures.

Whatever it was, we were soon playing pranks and getting into trouble. We lit a hillside near our subdivision on fire. Smoked pot and did other drugs. Several times I went to jail, once for possession of cocaine. My father had to come down and take me home. "I was in utter disbelief," says my father. "I didn't even know who my own son was." My mother didn't say much, she was too appalled.

When we started climbing, we were tripping. We were almost old enough to drive when half-a-dozen of us went to the old quarry, where we sat around, smoked dope, and hung out. During one lounge session one of my buddies pointed to the sandstone walls and said he'd seen some guy climbing it. "Oh, yeah," another said, and soon everyone was bumbling around on the rock, daring each other to go higher. We were grappling edges, smearing ribbed dishes in a dusty frenzy of Nikes, Vans, and Chuck Taylor All Stars.

A few months later, after a drawn-out begging session, my dad bought me a pair of EBs, the top climbing shoe of the day. "This doesn't mean I support climbing," he said. "I just think it's safer if you have the right shoes."

Those EBs became my prize possession. Cade Lloyd, soon to be my inseparable friend, followed suit a week later and together we climbed in the quarry almost daily for a year. Climbing rock felt powerful. Maintaining focus and rising to the challenge despite gave us a small inkling of self-worth.

Cade, myself, and to a lesser extent our peers, saw the lack of substance in our middle-class values. Caught between my parent's domestic conflict that nearly ended in divorce, I felt let down, rejected, and alienated. I saw the values espoused by my parents as hypocrisy. My mother's cancer tore open a huge emotional wound. I was unable to cope with it. If anything, the cancer merely interceded to save the inevitable breakup. Cade and I saw academic pursuits as a dead end — heavy on implication yet bereft of substance and accountability.

Occasionally, one of us would have a girlfriend, but we were too restless for any lasting relationship. We smoked too much pot, which turned from a soothing balm to an addiction that destroyed our ability to cope and communicate. My first girl-friend, an energetic redhead, was appalled when I mumbled something about "Spending more time with my bros" and broke up with her.

Bad things happened to Cade and me. The lack of core values and the sense of rootlessness led to confusion, wasted years, and sometimes tragedy. A climber friend was killed in a shoot-out with police. Another friend fell off a roof during a drunken pool-diving session. We were so stoned he lay on the concrete untreated and unnoticed until the paramedics arrived, choking on vomit. He was declared dead on the spot. The medics were disgusted.

Learning to climb in a relative vacuum created some perilous moments. Boise in 1979 was a climbing backwater in an era that predated indoor gyms. We spent the early 1980s practicing the techniques of the 1960s. Robbin's *Basic* and *Advanced Rockcraft* were our manuals. We hung on every word and could quote a passage like gospel when a question arose. Despite our encyclopedic knowledge of outdated techniques, we still managed to contrive complete epics.

With a few of our friends, Cade and I developed our anchoring skills by setting rappels and topropes. We started with slings around horns and trees. One of us had an 140-foot army-surplus Goldline rope. The kinky cable had a huge stretch. Eventually, Cade got a real rope and the Goldline was finished. It ended up being stretched to death a few years later, towing a car.

As our ambitions grew so did our need for climbing gear. Taking heed of *Basic Rockcraft*, we jammed knotted slings into cracks and threaded machine nuts we found in garages. Hardware surfaced from the strangest sources. One day Cade came up with some tapered welding wedges he'd found in an old factory building. Confident in his new find, he slung the wedges with webbing. Voila, homemade pitons.

Cade was always handy with gizmos. He once showed up with a zipgun made from an old spring and various plumbing parts. It shot .22 rimfires. He swore it worked great inside of five feet. Outside that range, the bullet tended to tumble. I never fired it for fear it might explode.

The welding wedges were soon taking a beating in all available fissures. The acid test came on a knifeblade crack in the quarry. Cade nailed several in a row, but the blunt wedges didn't punch in deeply enough. Cade ripped a whole string of them and went 20 feet to the deck. After six months of minor accidents and hair-raising gear failure, Cade scored some real stuff: a kernmantle rope, eight hexes and 10 carabiners.

We had the gear, yet setting anchors and belaying was still a great mystery. We started climbing at the Black Cliffs, the basalt crags lining the Boise River. I led the classic 5.9+ handcrack, the *Doug Scott Route*. (Local legend had it that British alpinist, Doug Scott had pioneered the route during a lecture tour.) At the time, it was a fearsome route with an oversized reputation. I heaved over the top, happy with my effort and bursting with pride. Up to that point, we'd exclusively employed hip belays. None of us had ever used a belay plate, and we never fell. Sitting on top of the *Doug Scott Route* was one of the first times I'd ever belayed a free pitch from the top. My second, a nice guy named Mike Rainey, tried following the pitch, and fell below the crux. The rope, running pulley style through a single unlocking biner scorched through my hands. Mike fell to the deck, mercifully low enough to avoid a crippling injury. He promptly quit climbing.

6

My new nickname, "Running Belay" lasted for six months.

We eventually amassed a good collection of nuts and pins, though some were antique even back then. We had a rack of Foxheads, primitive aluminum wedges swaged with a floppy cable. We also sported Peck crackers, round nuts of limited value. Once, I bought a full set of Forrest Titons, T-shaped nuts that fell out of their placements as often as they stayed put. Luckily, they were stolen a few months later. Soon, I too, had a kernmantle rope. We were ready to push the threshold of our own ignorance.

Our first lead climbs were moderate 40-foot cracks or tedious aid lines. Because 40 feet of climbing represented an all day effort for us, whoever drew belay duty was forced to find comfort in a jumble of flat rocks 10 feet from the base. We didn't know about placing directional anchors, and one day Cade went up slotting Stoppers in a vertical crack. Thirty feet up he fell and the rope, running at a diagonal from the climb to me over on the flat rocks, zippered every nut from the bottom up, save one — the top one.

After three days attacking that crack we finally lassoed the summit tree, a gnarled sage. In the grand style of the 1960s, the second followed, re-climbing the pitch on toprope. Each pin and nut placement was replaced, stood on, and back cleaned (later we discovered prussik knots). At the summit parking area we shook hands, proud as Everest summiteers.

The crazed streak pervading our lives never departed. It was sublimated, melding with climbing. One fall day Cade and I took LSD and bouldered for hours in the quarry. Acid-laced momentum drove us up a difficult new problem, a long-standing unclimbed shallow inside corner, bisected by a sloping shelf. Cade and I giggled our way over the top several times. The series of palmy slaps wasn't repeated for weeks despite the concerted effort of almost every local climber. That evening we slam danced in a crowded north-end basement to the blaring Dead Kennedy's, Circle Jerks, and Suicidal Tendencies. We could see the air vibrate to the bass line and we threw our bodies into the visible rhythm. On the way home we stopped in a graveyard. Inspired, I grappled with a six-foot high tombstone that bore a striking resemblance to the Washington Monument. The unanchored pillar fell over and broke my left leg. Cade drove me home on back of his Yamaha 250 Enduro.

My father wasn't pleased. He kept asking me "Why did you do it?" I couldn't tell him because I didn't know myself. On the way to the emergency room, I sat in the car in silence. The ER doctor wouldn't believe I was trying to do something as absurd as climbing a tombstone, and wanted to know who pushed it over.

A month later, in a walking cast, I was bouldering. I'd fall, land on one leg and collapse to the ground. A few weeks later the entire cast was gone and things were back to normal. While I was out of commission, Cade came over to borrow my rope. I wouldn't loan it to him partly out of youthful spite and partly because we lived by some old mountaineering adage about never loaning a rope. He didn't care. Cade went and soloed a local crack climb on aid with a 20-foot piece of webbing. An anemic rack led to some dicey placements. Halfway up, a Stopper blew, sending him on a spine-compressing fall onto the not so dynamic webbing belay. Deep down I was psyched because Cade joined me on the injured list, if only for a week.

As high school wore on so did the mental, physical, and emotional attrition rate. My friend Paul, a kid genius, built a bomb and blew a bank of lockers through the ceiling of our high school. It was toward the end of our senior year. Luckily no one was hurt. The victim was Paul. The police showed up at school and asked for him. Paul left his textbook and folder as if he was coming right back. He never returned.

As a senior, I did a few decent things. One was winning a state title in a debate tournament. For almost three years, I struggled through my debate class. I never won anything. But by the time my senior year rolled around, I'd gained enough street savvy to trade influence in the hallowed committees of the Idaho State Speech Tournament. I won first place as Outstanding Presiding Officer in the Idaho State Student Congress. My classmates were shocked. To them, I was just another stoner. When I received my trophy I didn't disappoint them — I was higher than 15 hippies at Woodstock.

Regardless of curricular success, climbing was so big a part of our identity that graduation night we dropped acid and bouldered on the local rocks.

After high school, I attended the University of Idaho in Moscow.

My parents wanted me to join the military. I wanted to "go to Yosemite and be a climbing bum." The notion didn't sit well. The U of I was a compromise — and an expensive one. I spent most of my time partying or climbing on the South Annex of the University's Art and Architecture building. Once I was even accosted at gun-point by the campus police who thought I was breaking in.

I got into more mischief. One night I was caught jimmying a candy machine with a coat hanger. I gave a false name. That got me into deeper trouble. A few weeks later I went before the Student Judicial Board. They were merciful despite my sketchy past and put me on probation. Earlier in the year, I made the front page of the college paper for being the only guy caught for possession of a controlled substance during a raid on Chrisman Hall. Reports of rampant drug use had put our resident hall on report to the local police. The actual raid coincided with a drug drought. No one was holding. I was caught because a residue of hash, wrapped in cigarette cellophane, was sitting at the bottom of my trash can. Someone had tossed it in unbeknownst to me. I was lucky to escape expulsion.

Not all was bad. I flunked sciences but scored A's in English and Humanities. I climbed at Leavenworth and the Peshastin Pinnacles. Though of modest stature, these crags were captivating. They were better than anything I'd seen and I hoped to climb such rock on a regular basis. But first, I had to establish a "real life" — or so I thought.

I dropped out after two semesters and was soon attending college back in Boise. A year later, Cade got in trouble with the law and went to the marines. On his return, after an early discharge, Cade left for the endless road-trip. He landed in Yosemite. Meanwhile, I interned at the local PBS station as a camera man and moonlighted as a busboy in an Italian restaurant. About then my mother died after her long bout with cancer. She passed on, uncertain of her youngest son's future and unable to help him. Youngsters blame themselves for everything. Guilt drove me into further depression. I sought surrogate fellowship in the local alternative music scene. I listened to hard-core and whittled away my days. Soon I realized I'd have to get out or go insane.

In 1985 I began dating a girl whose father lived in Fresno. She suggested that we move to California. I quit college and after a blowout with my father, packed up and left for Fresno. As soon as we got there my girlfriend dumped me. I packed up again and landed in the promised land of Yosemite Valley. I lived there for six years, and didn't speak to my father for the first three of those years. I went climbing and never looked back.

Bumbly goes big walling

Or, how I got my name

Arriving in Yosemite at 23, I not only had no illusions about career or higher education, I felt I had squandered the best years of my life. Landing in Yosemite Valley was the beginning, however, of my other education.

In August 1986 I was hanging out in Boy's Town near Curry Village, located in the gloomy east end of the Valley. I hadn't yet gotten a job, and spent my time bumming around, crashing on employee tent floors, rock climbing, and being a derelict.

Back then, the aspirant Valley local had two general roads to choose from. One was the path of the Free Climber; further down that road were specialization and the appropriate classification: hot crack climber, slab master (a dubious title), boulderer, steel-nerved free soloist, and so on. The second road was that of Big Wall Master. At the time, big-wall climbing was less in vogue than it is today, or had been in the 1960s and 1970s. Aid climbing was considered as a way to avoid the real deal — free climbing. Traffic was so light on the *Nose* that in peak season you could find yourself the only party on the route.

My free climbing improved, though not fast enough for my liking. I decided to hedge my bet with a little big-wall climbing. Since childhood, I had dreamed of climbing a big wall — if only once. I looked across the valley from Curry Village and there was the perfect first wall, the *South Face* of Washington Column. The *South Face* is the classic introductory Grade V wall

11

with 11 pitches of moderate clean aid and free climbing. My partner was a fellow floor hopper, Bill Kerwin. Bill was keen on doing the Column as his first big-wall outing, too. His talents complemented mine. He was burly where I was frail. He was sensible where I was flighty. He was bold where I was timid. Plus he had all the gear. Now that I think about it, I was a liability before we even started.

Bill and I got going early. The approach took us across meadows bathed in the pale blue half-light of early morning. We jugged ropes we'd fixed the day before to the huge bivy spot called Dinner Ledge. Bill led the next pitch, a 5.6 crack leading up to the Kor Roof, a jutting plane of blank granite leading over the lip to a Friend crack. The roof goes via three bolts, and is pretty straightforward to lead and clean, providing you have average common sense and a bit of wall savvy. Bill had what it took. He swarmed up the roof and made the belay in half an hour. I eagerly followed on jumars, arriving at the roof about 9 a.m. We were well on schedule for our projected 12-hour ascent.

Two hours later, I was still between bolt number one and bolt number two, perplexed. I'd passed jug school two days earlier at the Le Conte boulder, a 20-foot lump of granite garnished with a bolt ladder, yet somehow, on Kor's Roof, I couldn't move. I was back-tied three times and clipped with daiseys to both bolts. One jumar had mysteriously come unclipped from my body, and now sparkled in the afternoon sun on Dinner Ledge, 50 feet below. Bill finally snapped.

"What the hell is going on down there?" he yelled.

"Just a second," I yelled back.

I was tired and embarrassed. The situation was too complex to explain. I defrigged and rappelled. Bill rappelled, forced to leave a pricey string of cams above the roof. He said nothing.

We returned to Boy's Town that evening. Our so-called mates had been watching us through binoculars from the Curry Deck. Our demise, especially my slapstick contribution, gave them an event to celebrate on par with a New Year's Eve. Bill's reluctance to blame me in the face of gushing slaggery is a monument to his character. His only shortfall, actually, was climbing with me.

We went to bed early, intent on going back the next morning. Same plan. Knock off the *South Face* in 12 hours and be back on the Curry deck in time to diss our slacker friends.

This time, I led the roof pitch, which went without a hitch. Redeeming myself with a display of bravado on this easy A1 crack, I back cleaned with gusto, leaving large spaces between placements above the roof. The crack, however, paralleled the roof lip. That meant that every time Bill cleaned those spaced pieces he'd take a rope-grating swing and plummet out of sight. At the belay, he grabbed the rack, face livid. He said nothing and started up the leftward-leaning fifth pitch. After 50 feet he swung over and disappeared around the corner.

I relaxed, taking in the wind, the birds, and the heady ambiance of big-wall climbing. Here I was, living the dream. Abruptly, the realization dawned that I had not improved my jumaring since yesterday. How would I handle the complexities of cleaning the leaning corner and pendulum? I got up to the pendulum O.K., though for some reason I was running a 5.12 pump (my jugs were apparently set up for mandatory one-arm chins.)

The pendulum point was a fixed pin. Below was a #3 Friend. I knew nothing about lowering out. For long moments I agonized over the possibilities. I executed the only option. I grabbed the Friend, unclipped from the pin, and let go. I rattled across the face and looked back. Ten feet out right, Bill's brand new #3 Friend remained in the crack, complete with a shiny Chouinard 'biner.

The next pitches dragged by slowly. Easy Stopper cracks took forever. I couldn't get the placements more than three feet apart, and kept getting tangled in the mess of nylon straps, hardware, and rope. The August sun and 96-degree heat roasted us. Our water ran out. The two candy bars I'd brought were inedible without water to wash them down, and I was also cotton-mouthed with fear.

Bill cleaned one of my leads and muttered, "Try getting up in your second steps more often." He continued, "Not every placement has to be absolutely bomber. You should have used the #3 Friend in that pod. It would have saved you from dorking around with those nuts. Where'd the Friend go, anyway?"

"Hmmmm, let's see," I muttered. "You didn't drop it, did you?"

The route kicked back into lower-angle free climbing. The sun arced across the sky with alarming speed, fading from scorching white to burning yellow, and finally dipping into an orange horizon as we topped out. An hour later we were fighting through the tangled manzanita forest in a vain attempt to locate the infamous North Dome Gully. I recalled, on a continuous loop in my brain, that the guidebook said the gully was the scene of frequent accidents and that it traversed above death slabs: "If unfamiliar with the descent, don't attempt it at night."

My headlamp died — I'd neglected to change the battery after spending night after night reading route descriptions. Bill plugged away, weaving us down indistinct paths, avoiding dead ends, and rescuing us from a few cul-de-sacs. Around 11 p.m. I toppled over.

"C'mon, Pete. Get up," Bill said.

I said nothing. I was sleeping.

Bill tried a different technique, "If you don't get moving, we are going to die!"

His ruse failed. I was busy dreaming of large Cola Slurpees from 7-11.

Bill and I straggled back to Boy's Town the next morning. We buried our heads in the trough-like communal sink and sucked water like pigs. That day I rambled about, feeling the need to talk about the experience, sold on the buzz. I walked through the dusty rows of canvas tents and ran into one of the crew, a young climber named Matt Trent. He was sitting on a lawn chair in shorts and sandals. He strummed a guitar.

"Wanna hear a song," he smiled.

"Sure." I sat down and listened.

Matt curled over the guitar, opening with a bluesy measure that would have drawn tears from a Deadhead.

Then came the lyrics.

"This is the ballad of Bailin' Bill and Big Wall Pete.

"Two guys, tryin' to climb a wall — where they met defeat ..."

I stood up and walked off. Matt's singing faded into laughter.

Bill's nickname never stuck. For some reason mine did. I still cringe every time I see my nickname in print. But then I have to laugh, and think, what's in a name?

First published in Climbing *No. 179, September 1998.*

Up against the wall

In search of purpose on
El Cap

Up and down, up and down. Violent rocking, savage ripping. Feet are tangled in unyielding straps. Teeth are clenched in pained focus.

Bull riding? Motocross? Bondage? No. I've been thrown from my portaledge by a 70-mph wind gust. Snow and rain blow up, then sideways, then down. The ropes are tangled, writhing with a crazy arrhythmic passion. Sodden loops of nylon whack at my neighbor's portaledges. The four haulbags thrash about, possessed by some strange force. Below, Jeff occupies the only haven in this micro-hell. I must untie and unclip my anchor to start the perilous journey to my new home, a single Fish portaledge, currently inhabited and verging on ruin. The terrible void yawns below.

Tucker was drunk. It was late winter. Short days, wet weather, no current significant other. No visions, no revelations, no end in sight. No escape from a ghetto social scene, Bombay gin, and creeping despondency.

My lot was fairer. A recent trip to Hueco tanks under the tutelage of Russ "The Fish" Walling had left my life (and car) a wreck. I will only say that the diminutive Asian (myself) can be hard pressed to emulate the robust cornfed types. The fleshier ones seem to be able to drink in greater volume and duration. The net result of this winter bash at Hueco was an extended mandatory sojourn to the Valley, and a serious reconsideration of "what's it all about."

"Tucker, we gotta get to the big mountains," I said. "The big-ass granite walls." Switching to my most genteel voice, I paraphrase Yvon Chouinard: "We must venture forth to challenge the great granite faces of the world. We must train ourselves to endure the intense suffering that is the prerequisite to any great work of art."

My mouth was working overtime — the usual shit-talking poser stuff. Nothing new. But for once, Tucker actually concurred. Next, we agreed that to act as an effective team, we needed to climb difficult routes together. Jeff joined us for a beer, and we enlisted him in our fantasy expedition. The night dragged on. We drank with fervor to forget the dreary present. We ranted and raved and planned. We would do a training route in the spring, then El Cap's *Aurora* in late fall.

Aurora was a fine candidate for an adventure — overhang, sustained, and technically difficult, it had seen very few ascents. Taking a line on the monolith's southeast face, *Aurora* was first climbed in the fall of 1981 by Greg Child and Peter Mayfield. The rating is VI 5.10 A5, and even after four ascents the route has retained its reputation as a scary heads-up undertaking. Pitch seven (the crux) had scored two 100-foot falls. Pitch 12 ascends the "Gong Flake," a huge radically expanding feature hanging menacingly above the belay, poised to kill both the leader and belayer. At a holiday party in El Portal I quizzed Mayfield about the Gong Flake. "Oh, it's still there?" was his surprised response. Telescopic scrutiny, though, had provided us proof of the flake's tenuous existence. Added to the technical difficulty was the threat of late-season weather. Some practice walls would be crucial. Our November jump-off date would give me an entire Valley season to ditch my sport-climbing obsession and focus on getting up Big Walls.

But 10 partners, eight walls, two serious storms, one Grade IV first ascent, and 30 wall bivys later, I was burned out and dreading *Aurora*. Enough was enough. I wanted to hangdog on trusty bolts. I wanted to wear sticky slippers and tight trousers. But my whining fell upon callous ears. The plan was the plan. No deviation.

16

Strategy, preparation, and logistical hassles are often more time-consuming than the actual climbing. The bigger the project, the bigger the workload. *Aurora* demanded coordinating four people's conflicting schedules and collecting a large amount of gear. The headaches of preparation could make a whole separate story. Short days, potentially serious weather, and the sheer size of "Team *Aurora* " doubled the normal wall loads. Our haulbags would eventually tip the scales at 300-plus pounds.

Tucker Tech was my wall-climbing teacher, and was often amused by my epic antics. Tucker's confidence in my ability was such that he once stated, "I would sooner beat you on the head, stuff you in a haulbag, and drag your sorry ass up as climb any wall route with you." Like many of his Search and Rescue teammates, Tucker can be brutally honest, raving drunk, and downright rude. His sympathy and benevolence can be startling during their rare appearances.

I have also seen Tucker silently endure pain and anguish. During the third ascent of El Cap's *Lost World,* Tucker and I encountered a freezing storm that lasted several days. Retreat was impossible and our bivy gear was less than adequate — homemade "K-mart" portaledges sans rainflys, no sleeping bags, and hand-me-down nylon parkas. During this sobering, trial in which we spent 36 hours shivering in pools of ice water, I came to admire Tucker's stoicism and tenacity.

Highlighting Tucker's career is a five-week-big-wall solo binge — triggered by a sour relationship — during which he knocked off four El Cap routes. "I wanted to destroy every last grain of emotion," he said later. "I wanted nothing more than to feel nothing." Looking at his long list of achievements, which includes countless first ascents and perhaps 30 Grade VI wall climbs, one can only wonder how much pain Tucker has encountered.

Jeff Perrin is a fellow Curry Company employee. He is the most even-tempered guy I have ever know, and generous beyond all expectations. His relaxed attitude seems to verge on carelessness at times; sometimes I feel that he flat out doesn't give a shit. For example, Jeff dropped the entire food bucket during a late fall ascent of *Mescalito.* One PowerBar per day barely saw us through the remaining six days of our trip. His cavalier outlook propels him up hard aid pitches at breakneck speed, while his recent six-day solo of El Cap's *Zenyatta Mendatta* epitomizes his boldness.

Greg Epperson, Epi, Epps, or the Epps Machine. His name is synonymous with distinguished climbing photography, and he is a nice guy. Epi had never done a wall; however, his drive to pursue his craft manifests itself in joining crazy projects like *Aurora*. Epi's role was that of photographer/documenter. He was in for nice ride.

The three of us now gaze slack-jawed at the 600-foot static rope hanging free from *Aurora's* sixth-pitch belay. We have set the stage with three days of climbing steep, streaked granite. "This shit is nuts," I say. "Only the biggest idiots would fix this high. There's no reason for it." Fear emerges in the form of complaint. The thought of free-air jumaring the line 60 feet out from the wall is more than slightly disconcerting.

The others pulled a neat stunt yesterday by counterweight hauling our four fat bags to the belay. They had jugged to the high point while I loafed at the base, "haulbag packing." When the pulley and backup were ready Tucker and Epi acted as a counterweight and slowly lowered to the ground, with Jeff serving as the anchorman and slowing their descent with leather-clad hands.

Today, the trip up the line takes each of us at least 30 minutes of gut-churning, puke-inducing toil. "This rope is safe, this rope won't cut, I will never exert enough strain to cut this rope," is my mantra.

Repetitions count off as feet creep by, converting themselves into yards, and finally noticeable distances. Hoarse and sweat-soaked from the 80-degree November heat, I am relieved and quite please to clip the belay. My next challenge is to ready myself for the next lead. The wild jumar, the beating sun, and my parched mount cause me to gag as I look up. While prepping the rack I light up a Camel to calm my nerves.

Pitch seven, the "American Zone," is 150 feet long, circuitous, overhanging, and rated 5.10 A5. Mike O'Donnell and Chuck Clance have both lobbed for 100 feet off the pitch. Through the telescope the stone had appeared blank. Up close the American Zone is a series of thin flakes and grooves separated by unlikely expanses of streaked granite. Under my breath, I mutter, "nuts, yeah, Friends, yeah, pins, yup, heads, yo, hooks? for sure."

I'm ready for action. No stalling. "Be careful. You can die up there," encourages Jeff. The madness begins. An arrow, a #2 Camalot, then the first in a series of fixed copperheads. I am a bit leery of the heads because they're six to 10 years old. Furious bounce testing for the next 30 feet insures that the gear can withstand a minimal shock load. The head wires poke out at crazy angles. Feet barely touch the wall as my weight pulls the wire almost perpendicular to the stone, twisting at the beaten copper. Chouinard hook next, OK. Two Leeper points in succession. What next? I hear something. I look down. Tucker has finally made it up after a leisurely breakfast at the Ahwahnee Hotel. We exchange unpleasantries. My own meltdown asserts itself.

Hooking has taken me 15 feet above the last of the copperheads. It is a fair certainty that the successive blobs of battered metal will not arrest a 30-foot fall. Consequently, a mistake could result in a 100-footer. It is in my best interest to treat the next placement with respect and care. I crank into the substeps of my aiders and strain to daisy in tight. The angle is so kooky that the base legs of the Leeper pointed hook do not touch the face while its tiny point creaks back and forth. I search vainly for the obvious, the inobvious, and finally, the non-existent.

Above is the ledge. It is perhaps a foot wide, promising, maybe even hookable. If I could but latch the ledge then maybe I could get something to stick. A tiny flake! It is minuscule, barely within straining reach, hollow to the tap. It might take a hook ... The Chouinard hook comes off the rack. I carefully clip it to my aiders which in turn are attached to one of my daisies. Gingerly, I set the hook edge on the meager flake, and pull down on the daisy. The flake creaks. The hook digs in and sinks. Gritting my teeth, I squint my eyes and slowly ease a foot into the aider step. I delicately transfer pressure from the Leeper point onto the Chouinard hook.

"Cool! This piece of shit's gonna actually hold," I think. Just stay put for a few more sec ..."

CRACK. The flake snaps and I am falling.

Adrenalin jolts my body. The fall of a lifetime is cut short by the pointed Leeper hook lodged to stone by a few millimeters of chrome-moly steel. Good thing I'm light. Through the haze I can hear Tucker explaining some jive about the pitch. He seems to know more about what is happening than I do. "Typical Tucker Tech," I mutter.

I down aid to a lower hook and shorten the Leeper's sling to a minimum. Placing it again, I strain into the high steps, and, using a right-hand edge for balance, slip my feet out of the aiders. "Slack," I yell. "I'm free climbing."

My feet paw for purchase on the slick brown stone. Groping at full extension, my left hand catches a sloping hold. I smear a wrinkle with my right toe, then slide my left hand an inch higher. No longer weighted, the Leeper hook drops to the end of my daisy chain and swings to and fro. Now both feet bicycle as I mantel onto the ledge. The rope drag, haul line, and rack conspire to pull me back into the void. But a high-step and friction rock-over put me eye-to-eye with an A1 pin placement. I mutter thanks to God and my FiveTennies. A few more hours of heading lands me at a rivet. I lower to the belay, the pitch half completed.

The most severe artificial pitch of my life ends the next day after nine total hours.

The ensuing pitches vary in character, yet each ropelength merges with the next to shape the greater continuity. The features mingle, building a sheer mosaic, bold vertical black, red bursts, and white highlights on a golden backdrop. The canvas extends in all directions, a dramatic stage for an intense drama. At belays I am awed by *Aurora's* meandering path, a passage that links fragile features. The route is a thin line, tenuous, vulnerable, and wildly beautiful.

Jeff and Tucker make short work of their leads. Greg plies his trade with impressive calm. He is neither gripped by the exposure nor alarmed by his teammates' emotional flares. Team *Aurora* plods along in harmony, sharing humor, happy to be at work.

We are closing in fast on the Gong Flake, which we have christened "Tucker's Last Pitch Ever." Day three starts with pitch 11, Jeff's lead. The topo indicates two A4 sections, thus Tucker and I allow for a day of rest and relaxation. However, in a frenzied display of speed and finesse, Jeff blitzes to the belay in little more than two hours. His rapid lead includes a stretch of 13 consecutive heads and sporty hooking. Tucker and I have been taken by surprise. We are in the midst of our rest-day party when the bad news dawns on us. Tucker will die when the colossal meat cleaver pulls and cuts the rope. I will be sliced off the wall. Perhaps Tucker could ride the plate like a granite surfer, arrive at the base unscathed, and be in the Mountain Room Bar tonight. Not. Resigned to certain doom, Tucker jugs the trail line while I sadly clean the pitch.

Tucker hooks off a river and raps the flake with his hammer. *Gong ... gong ... gong.* I cringe. He drives an arrow to the eye with three gentle taps. "Yep, it's expando all right," he says. I'm too drunk to be scared and so is he. Tucker continues, placing TCUs and pitons that expand the granite blade. Each placement widens the fissure, rendering the gear below useless. Tucker mounts a TCU. It slips, then barely catches. In desperation, he fumbles for a Friend. The wrong size. He fumbles and drops it. A hasty, Hail Mary hook on a crumbling outside edge temporarily defuses the bomb.

"Good thing that hook held because he was lookin' at a monster ripper, te he he," I think.

Tucker finishes the lead as the sun turns red in the west. By that time I am neither scared nor elated, just hung over.

When I start a wall climb, I address all fears. Like an army general studying the troops of his opponent, I scrutinize the enemy. I weigh technical aspects and approach objective hazards with great dread. I try to envision "worst possible scenarios," paying scrupulous attention to detail.

By the end of day five we have arrived at "the worst possible scenario." Having fixed to the end of pitch 13, we are three pitches from the summit, but the weather is going bad.

We have spent the morning hours holding our rainflys in a vain attempt to stay dry. We are reduced to a fragile nylon fortress, continually harassed by an invisible and persistent enemy. The rainflys billow like sails as the wind gusts, stretching the seams almost to the point of tearing. My hands are frozen and the stress exacts a free-climbing pump, relentless and punishing. As the rainflys billow our ledges rise turbulently and then hammer down as the wind ferociously reverses.

Jeff, occupying the lowest berth in our porta-city, is experiencing the worst of it. His free-hanging ledge lacks stability and kicks around in the wind, a testament to *Aurora's* steepness and a harbinger of impending calamity.

I pray, over and over, "Oh, God, just make it stop."

Hours go by. A brief lull permits conversation.

"What's the forecast?" I ask Jeff, who is fiddling with our radio (stolen from our manager at the Four Seasons Restaurant, Mike Gover).

"Forecast calls for pain," he yells back.

"More rain! More pain! ARRRRGGHH!" interjects Tucker, who has moved into Epi's double-wide ledge to take shelter under the rainfly. Epi quietly snaps off film. During a lull, I can hear the wind whistling off in the distance. Suddenly the silence is torn by a huge gust and my thin nylon shell billows, then rips with a scream. I see a nightmare of frozen ropes and wildly animated gear. Another gust tosses me up and sails me horizontal, like a human kite. Shocked, I manage to yell, "Check it out. It's rodeo time!"

I feel like I could untie and fly to the summit. The nylon straps are wrapped around my legs, literally holding me horizontal in the 70-mph blasts. The ledge flaps violently about, threatening to smash my neighbors' heads and destroy their shelters. With my knife I frantically cut the whole flying mess loose. Tucker's abandoned ledge is next to go. The cots streak off, eventually disappearing around The Nose. I swing to Jeff's portaledge feet first. He grabs my legs and hauls me into his sodden home.

Jeff writes in his journal:

"This is going to be a very long night. There is so much rattling and swinging. This is ghetto. Pete calls it burial at sea. This is way ghetto."

Jeff and I set, clenching the rainfly on a portaledge built for one person. Jury-rigging an elaborate system of cut slings and soggy knots allows us a free hand. We each fire a shot of tequila. The warming rush comforts our hearts and soothes our taut nerves. We shake hands across soaked bivy sacks.

"Here's to the business," Jeff toasts.

"Yeah, this sure sucks. What's the forecast?" I ask.

Jeff smiles. "Forecast calls for pain."

We lie side by side in a space designed for one. Any movement is painful and the extremities grow numb with cold. Icy tendrils of water and wind torture our contorted bodies. My mind wanders, a hand comes unclasped from the rainfly and the wind gusts it up, snapping my drowsy brain into panicked reaction. The fly presses into my face. The wind eases. Night falls.

I am talking to my friend, Karine Nissen, who is standing in an immaculate, modern kitchen. White tile and radiant light embrace me with heat and comfort. Karine hands me a Peets Coffee catalog. "Pick one out," she says. I wander to the table and ease into the chrome and wicker chair. "This is real living," I say. Karine smiles serenely at me. A spotless coffee machine rests on the glass table, awaiting my whim. The thought of coffee slides my brain into neutral. I know everything is going to be okay. I sigh with pleasure. Drip — Drip — Drip — what's that. Drip — Drip — Drip. My pile jacket is leaking onto the floor. I look at my hands. They are wrapped in wet tape and sodden leather gloves. I notice my smell — damp and sour, like mildew. I realize my folly.

"Sorry, Karine, I've gotta go."

"Why?" she asks, concerned.

"I am leaving because I'm somewhere else and you are a dream."

The vision of Karine's face fades and I am sent roaring back into freezing, suffocating reality. My bladder is screaming for relief. My mouth is parched from dehydration. Jeff's feet are denting my head.

Icy mist streams through our lonely piece of the world. The dense clouds form a wall of darkness and opaque haze. Everything is frozen solid.

A distant voice calls, "Climbers on El Capitan, can you respond?"

Tucker, in the ledge above, stirs to life. "We are OK," he yells.

"We are okay, aren't we? he asks.

The voice in the meadow calls again, "Climbers on El Cap, do you need a rescue?"

At least someone cares. In union we yell that a rescue is not necessary. I wonder to myself, "How long can this go on before we do need one?" The night is endless. Once again, I find myself exhausted yet unable to sleep. Five-minute micro-dreams are interrupted by 10-minute nightmares of consciousness.

The next day the sun comes out and gives us a shot at the summit. It takes hours for the ropes to thaw. We hurriedly pack the gear and begin climbing through water streaks and falling ice. Time is of the essence. When night falls the ropes will refreeze. Another storm could be fatal. We must make the summit tonight.

Jeff leads a ladder and hook pitch into the last two ropelengths of *Tangerine Trip*. It is dark by the time Tucker finishes the next lead. The final lead is mine. At 11:30 p.m. I claw onto the frozen summit of El Capitan. My breath condenses, obscuring the frozen fairy tale landscape dancing in the flickering light of my dying headlamp. I crunch through shin-deep snow and anchor the lead line to a guarded tree. My boots are frozen solid. The rope is like lead.

Tucker comes up next. He stumbles past without saying a word. He seems to be looking for something. I think we all are.

First published in Climbing *No. 132, June 1992.*

Heavy Weather

Rejuvenation on El Cap's hallowed ground

At one time I felt possessed. I used to say, "I am my own god. I live life. Life doesn't live me." In trying to uphold my self-imposed slavery I created much pain, for myself and others. The only option was to run, a necessarily desperate endeavor. In the past I would flee to some crazy piece of rock.

The end nearly came in Yosemite Valley when I was struck by rockfall on Half Dome. Bill Russel and I were ascending a new line on the Northwest Face when a volley of rock streamed by. Thrill-seeking tourists had almost killed me. I felt helpless. The scars on my face and arm still remind me of my frailty.

On another escapade Tucker Tech and I reeled up toward the West Face of El Cap, half psyched to do a one-day ascent of *Realm of the Flying Monkeys*. After last call in the Mountain Room Bar we packed our bags and hiked to the base. Twenty-three hours later we wobbled to the top, and returned to the Valley Floor at four in the morning after a sleepless 47-hour "day." Stumbling alone through the pines, I was haunted by strange visions and a terrible whining, buzzing noise. Hallucination or glimpse of mystery? Was I hunting or being hunted?

Starvation, dehydration, fatigue, and fear — my ever-present wall playmates. No water and 120-degree heat on Leaning Tower.

A freezing storm on the *Triple Direct*. A frigid 36-hour bivouac on *Lost World*. A panicky midnight nightmare on *Vodka Putsch*.

These experiences were hiding places where torment was relief. One experience stands apart in its absurdity and still floats in my head as a strange dream.

This is the story of *Sunkist* and how we almost drowned on El Capitan in mid-July.

Sunkist first came to mind during the "Italian Nose Rescue" in 1990. Three ill-equipped Italians stalled on Camp Six just below the summit of El Cap. A nasty spring storm rendered the team immobile, and I ended up as a part of a park service rescue. During this ordeal, Tracy Dorton, a fellow rescuer and veteran of countless extreme nail-ups, mentioned *Sunkist* as one of the few routes worth climbing on the left side of El Cap. The left side has been referred to as "the ladies' side." In general, routes to the right of the *Nose* are steeper, scarier, and more committing than the ones on the other side. *Sunkist* was one of a few notable exceptions. At the time of the rescue, the big name and the daunting A5 grade were too scary. It was not until a year later that *Sunkist* became a real goal.

Sunkist is the work of Dale Bard and Bill Price. In 1978 the duo climbed what Bard later described as, "Probably the most mentally straining route ... you get so far off the ground you can't come down. It was questionable as to whether the crack systems were even there."

The route follows a traversing line below the *Shield* headwall, then punches through the solid gold wall left of *Magic Mushroom* via a series of beautiful thin cracks. The topo's rack list includes 25 RURPs, 25 knifeblades, 25 Lost Arrows, and 50 copperheads, indicating a delicate line. At one point a solitary crack splits the wall for several hundred feet, in one of the most compelling sheets of stone I have seen.

Jeff Perrin, my regular wall partner, was stoked to stroke his fetish for thin nailing. Our information on *Sunkist* ranged from sketchy second-hand reports to dubious rumors. From the limited data, we guessed our party to be the fifth ascent team.

Greg Epperson, one of the few professional photographers who has shot wall climbing up close, was keen on getting the best photos possible. I thought our earlier epic on *Aurora* would have been enough to scare the daylights out of him, but his search borders on obsession. "Epi" continued to photograph other El Cap routes, refining his technique with each new project. On previous trips, Epi was limited to the belay for most of the action, and he wanted more versatility in shooting angles and freedom from the climbing team.

Epi had a new plan for *Sunkist.* In a remarkable burst he hiked up the backside of El Cap with 2000 feet of rope, intending to fix the upper two-thirds of the route. His first whack at rappelling *Sunkist* ended 200 feet below the rim and 400 feet to the right of the climb. I spied his blunder from the meadow via telescope, and laughed at the magnitude of his error. Locating the top-out points of climbs is a difficult feat on the rounded, indistinct summit rim. My laughter faded when I imagined the labor needed to correct his error. True to form, Epi retraced his steps, bivied on top, then moved his ropes and rappelled 2000 feet to Mammoth Terraces the following day. From there he descended a motley selection of old fixed lines for another 800 feet to the base. Never before had anyone gone through so much pain to document an ascent of El Cap.

After the Aurora climb, I soloed *Zodiac* in mid-December. The climb was classic and graced with wonderful warm weather. After *Zodiac,* I ran out of steam. The escape value of wall climbing was wearing thin.

Sport climbing and an ever-growing passion for Christianity occupied my life. I became a full believer. The word "Christian" can evoke many images in the non-believer's eye. To me it always used to represent hypocrisy, lies, and kookiness. I cannot speak for or about others. I can only say that I believed. With that comes hardship, responsibility, failure, and joy.

My faith does not hinge on ideology, theology, or doctrine. It is simply belief in Christ and his teachings. When I attend church, I sometimes disagree with the message or the manner in which the message is presented. Yet I cannot dismiss the Divine.

Some may look at my life and say, "What a sad example of a Christian he is." They are probably correct. I have a long way to go, but I have no regrets. It is as it is. Belief compels me to see the world afresh, replete in its beauty and ugliness. *Sunkist* became an opportunity to revisit the world of El Capitan and experience it anew. Everything changes through Christ, even apparently minuscule details of one's existence. I dread the pain of change, yet change I must. I dreaded *Sunkist*, but curiosity and a strange surety of purpose inexorably drew me.

It had been nearly six months since either Jeff or I had been on El Cap. During that time both of us dealt with the ebb and flow of life, and Jeff's direction often seemed counter to mine. As the world faded for me, Jeff seemed to be more enamored with its alluring accessories.

The rigors of preparation were more bothersome than usual. Perhaps we had a premonition, or maybe we were just lazy. Wall prep is like getting ready for a family vacation. Phone calls must be made, arrangements to cover the multitude of petty details are a must. Stress levels rise, tempers can flare, and the entire routine of life is disrupted. After a good week of wire-snapping tension, we were off. We were relieved when the actual climbing began.

If Jeff and I were running a business we would quickly go bankrupt. Epi, on the other hand, was always efficient. The morning of day one was no exception. A series of silly delays (Jeff forgot his ascenders in El Portal at his girlfriend's house, another hour round-trip) put us off schedule.

When we flopped down at the base of the climb, Jeff sulked. "She stood me up last night," he blurted. "I'm going up on the big stupid stone grade and she stands me up. I can die up there and she stands me up."

I rolled my eyes. Her full name, I forget. Her first was Sarah. We dubbed her, "Sarah Conner" after the heroine of *The Terminator.* She was a teenager, pretty, and probably very nice. Her character I cannot attest to, but one thing was guaranteed: Jeff would carry a female millstone around his neck for the entire climb.

In his finest Schwarzenegger monotone, Epi thundered, "SARAHH CAANAAHH?"

Jeff flinched.

"Do you love her?" I asked.

"She's OK."

"Did you get what you wanted, Jeff?"

"Nope, like Tucker says, I get what I deserve."

Halfway through haulbag packing I realized I had forgotten much of my food. The trip back to the truck burned an another hour. Jugging the six ropelengths to Mammoth Terraces took the rest of the day. Once again Jeff demonstrated his uncanny ability to deal with big loads. He took it upon himself to jumar with not one, but two full haulbags suspended from his harness. Not to be mistaken for an effeminate artsy type, Greg proved to be one gutsy, load-humping enigma.

It was evening when we finally set up our bivy. Mammoth Terraces is a huge ledge system and the staging point for several routes. Above us rose the great Shield headwall, and to the left spread the solid-gold sea of *Sunkist.*

Tucker told me that he had seen it snow in Yosemite every month of the year. I didn't believe him. My Valley residence of five years had been characterized by hot summers and dry winters. These were drought years and the only time it seemed to storm was when I was on walls.

"*Sunkist* in July must be safe," I exclaimed in a moment of fool-ishness. "It's boiling hot. I'm not even going to bring bivy gear, just my sleeping bag." Later, however, I sheepishly packed some storm gear, hoping my rash words would be forgotten. The sky soon darkened and clouds moved in. There was a fresh bite to the air that was uncharacteristic of July.

The next morning, Jeff led the first pitch, a broken 5.8 crack. I put away the next pitch of quick A1. We hauled the loads up unco-operative slabs and reracked for the next step. Jeff cruised the following pitch, A1. The fourth A3-rated pitch turned out be a very short A1 with some free moves. On the fifth lead of the day, Jeff padded up a short corner in his resoled Converse All Stars. From there he slung a detached block and lowered out of sight into another corner. A tension traverse and several awkward free moves landed him on a small needle of stone graced with two bolts. This was our new home. We set up house and ate. The ini-tial pitches were part of the *Magic Mushroom,* so up to this point we were in trade-route country. The difficulties to here seemed minor. The cracks were worn by many ascents, and fixed gear dan-gled in crucial parts. In a day we would embark into a land where few had climbed. That night it rained gently.

As I gazed at the next lead from my portaledge the following morning I felt at peace. Pitch six was rated A3. It began with tenuous nailing on brown granite through dramatic bulges. After 40 feet I pendulumed left into a thin dihedral. From that point I was forced to back-clean and trust tied-off blades and short shallow-angle pitons. A fall would have resulted in a 60-foot swing into a distant corner. This section was better than espresso, and the buzz sustained me through several RURPs and heads to the belay. I thought to myself, "God has given me peace, but that was still way scary."

Jeff was mad about his girl and seemingly the world in general. The next pitch, however, was the slap in the face he needed. Hook moves straight off the belay led to some old fixed heads. After 30 feet of insecurity, normalcy returned. The pitch ended in a rivet ladder followed by a short, expanding A2+ traverse. The next lead was short and uneventful, and a final mantle deposited me on a narrow, sloping ledge, which would be our residence for the next two days.

The process of starting a wall climb seems, for me anyway, to be the crux. The initial days are hard, as one leaves behind the comforts of home and enters an altogether different environment. It is during this transition (and I speak from painful experience) that the decision to go down or up is usually made. There's a Grateful Dead song that goes: "Well the first days are the hardest days, don't you worry anymore ... when life looks like easy street there is danger at your door." At this point on the climb our commitment was not total, yet we were well into "wall mode." Life was looking like "easy street."

I drilled rivets to hang our portaledges. It was clouding up again, but, "Hey, man, it's July." Our shelters were lined up in a row. Jeff and I soon perfected a system to dole out food, water, vodka, and other essentials. We hung the radio on a pin.

That evening a big Pacific storm system moved in, roaring like full-blast TV static. The rain pelted our flys in sheets. Water running off the summit coalesced into small cascades. From my position, I could hear a small waterfall start on Epi's side and gradually work its way down to me. It was like a giant was taking a wiz on our bivy, spraying us back and forth. Morning found us wet and getting wetter. I prayed for strength and patience. It wasn't that I was miserable, there were just other places I'd rather have been. During recent weeks I was drawn to the Yosemite Clinic, suffering from real and imaginary ailments. My thoughts drifted to the nurse I had been seeing. Ah, to be there now. ...

When the storm eased, we took stock of the situation.

"I'm completely soaked. How are you doing, Pete?" asked Jeff, wringing out his bag.

I smiled in the privacy of my tent and replied, "I'm pretty wet." A lie. I was merely damp. Even in a direct torrent, the rainfly of my top-secret Fish portaledge had deflected the water.

During the day, the rain dripped, poured, stopped, and dripped again. We would occasionally peer out from under sopping rain-flys at our little world. A Japanese team below was hurting. They were climbing below the Shield when the storm caught them on a low-angle groove system. Forty feet above them lay the rain shadow of the *Shield* Roof — dry ground. Now they were stuck in a huge drainage and the water was pummeling them. No manner of rainfly could provide protection under that beating. We had gleaned the name of one of their team from some gear they stashed on Mammoth Terraces. It was Eizo Mitani. Being unfamiliar with the others, we addressed our queries at him. Epi yelled, "Eizo!" Jeff and I shrieked our greetings. From far below the Japanese defiantly shouted back. If we were going to be cool, then they were too. The shouting brought a tear to my eye. We were all sharing a very intense experience, hidden from the rest of the world. And they were, after all, my people.

The night delivered more rain and more pain. A small river had developed under our ledges. The water lapped at the bottom of our beds and began to soak through. To compound matters, the only radio station we could get played the same inane songs ad nauseum. Some crazy band would scream every hour, "This is real ... this is now ... this is a freak show baby anyhow ..." Strangely appropriate, though.

The closer I get to someone the more I feel like I am looking in a mirror. Eventually, something in the other person becomes really offensive. I get angry, repulsed, and judgmental. In the midst of judgment, comes the realization that I am the one at fault.

Jeff pissed me off when he kicked my ledge. He had been bugging me and I only wanted to suffer in silence. I responded with a few choice expletives. Embarrassed, I diverted attention from my outburst.

"I'm sick of this view," I said. "Every time I come up here it's the same old thing. You got your big, stupid Cathedral Rocks ..."

"Yeah," Jeff interrupted, "those ugly low angle pieces of ..." His voice drifted as he recalled a nightmare on the *Direct North Buttress*. Jeff and John Pinchott had climbed the *DNB* in baking mid-summer heat. With their water long gone, Jeff was reduced to drinking from the tepid scum pool they found on top.

Paraphrasing one of our favorite passages from "A Letter Received by Steve Roper," published in *Games Climbers Play*, I continued: "So here we are climbing El Capitan looking like a few stupid beatniks."

Jeff picked it up, "Yeah, we can now rest on our laurels as the three pigs who climbed up the stone steep grade."

We broke into hysterics. The radio babbled. We drank more vodka. I dreamed of my nurse, and life was good.

Next morning, the sky showed signs of clearing. I was groggy even after 18 hours of sleep. For me, waking, eating, taking a dump, and breaking camp are the worst times on a wall. Day Four was especially agonizing after two days of immobility. Human nature tends to cling tenaciously to its current state, even if it stinks.

As we packed, a shout caught our attention. Team Japan was on the move. More than moving, they were running for their lives. The direct beating they took must have been far worse than ours. The usual catcalls and insults traditionally meted out to retreating teams were forgotten. Instead we shouted farewell, respectful of their grit and spirit.

The sky was almost clear when Jeff started pitch nine. A few hooks led to easier aid. Loose free climbing brought him to a belay below a roof. My lead of the day consisted of aiding and offwidthing a short but awkward chimney. The rock was damp and cold, yet we were exhilarated by the growing exposure and warmed by our exertions.

The top showed pitch 11 as a few black lines with the notation "A4." Jeff tapped up a flush crack to where it petered out. "This topo is wrong," he muttered. Where the topo showed one crack there were three. Faced with a dead end, Jeff decided to swing around for a better view. I lowered him and eased back to watch the show. Hanging from a tied-off blade he began to sprint back and forth. I could almost rail him a high five every time he came flying by. His first few swings were slightly tentative, respectful of the frail pendulum point. Respect gave way to frustration. Twice his hand grazed an edge and both times he came spinning back like a puppet, hammer flying, slings and haul line flailing. Anger flashed in his eyes. Girls, the rain, the world — all were enough to prod him on with a renewed vigor. He dug in, swung over, and barely lurched into a groove.

Jeff nailed a shallow dihedral, using the static haul line as a lead cord since the main rope shot horizontally across the wall, useless for protection. The aid placements were tenuous. I do not know what would have happened had he fallen.

Pitch 12 marked our entry into the zone of sheer gold. This was what we were after. The A4-rated pitch went at A3. Modern gear, technique, and attitude slid us through where our predecessors must have tiptoed. The following lead consisted of two short features connected by long rivet ladders. Jeff slipped TCUs behind flexing plates, where Price and Bard must have nailed. Modern gear dropped this pitch to A2.

But I gazed at the next pitch in awe. A delicate crack bisected the wall into identical halves. The line continued forever, and the belay bolts seemed a mile away. I threw most of our hardware onto the rack.

Fifty feet into the lead a noise caught my ear. It was Epi. He was dangling above, shadowing my movements. I kept forgetting he was there, mere feet away, yet in a world apart.

"Why, Greg? Why? Why are you doing this to us?" I pleaded in mock anguish, dangling from a knifeblade.

"I'm just using you guys for your skills and faces," he answered.

"Oh, yeah? If this blade blows, I'm going to grab your foot. Then we'll see who's using who."

"Go ahead, lurch away." Greg's face was hidden behind the

Nikon. His mouth produced words, yet he was strangely detached. His art was his sole focus. Sometimes he seemed only an apparition.

"Hey, Epi, you know if you spin that little dial with the little colored numbers the pictures will come out different?"

"Yeah, I know."

As I reached up to tie off the next blade, I muttered, "He's crazy."

The lead was 165 feet long and took gear from a #3 Camalot all the way down to a RURP. The Camalot fit into one of several rare pods. Otherwise, the crack was consistently thick knifeblades to tied-off baby angles. The final 20 feet tapered to a seam, demanding a bit of improvisation. Tipped blades and tied-off stacks got me within spitting distance of the belay. Epi's foot started to look like a Thank God bucket. Grab his foot, match, yell for slack, mantle his head and clip the belay. Nah. Instead, a #1 head (I had no proper pitons left on me) then the belay. Aid pitches don't get much better.

Clouds filled the sky as I completed the pitch. I was so absorbed that the falling mist did not register. But while setting up to haul I noticed a drop of rain. My raingear was neatly packed away in the sacks 165 feet below. No big deal, I thought, the wall is too steep for me to get wet. Besides it was July. My mind relaxed as I set up. My eyes took in the sheer exposure and the burnished rock. Few places on El Cap are so magnificent. The entire length and breadth of the left side of El Cap fanned out beneath us. Glorious. The rock at the belay was a shade browner and scabbier than the neighboring gold. Suddenly a wind gust snapped me into awareness. Sheets of rain were plunging to the Valley floor 20 feet out from the wall.

"Check it out," I said to Greg, laughing. "This is so killer. That stuff ain't even gonna hit us."

A few random drops hit my skin. They were big. I glanced up just in time to catch more beads in my face. Epi was fumbling with the hood of his jacket. "That bastard is always ready, just like some freakin' Boy Scout," I mused. Jeff was sitting at the belay below, with his head ducked under the haulbags. He must be dozing. I began the haul with a greater sense of urgency. My only insulation was a sweatshirt.

Earlier in the trip we had hauled in two loads; today we tried to haul everything at once, including the extra water for the hot weather we weren't getting. The bags barely budged. Shit. The drizzle turned into a downpour. I heard the volume rise a second before it hit me. Shit. I was getting soaked. Five days worth of dirt and sweat were washed from my matted hair and into my mouth. For all my frantic efforts, the bags were now only five feet higher.

The bags easily outweighed my meager 125 pounds. "Shit. This is what I get for being an anorexic sport climber."

Epi watched in silence. In desperation I sought shelter under his photographer's seat. No help. One hundred forty feet below Jeff was beating the pins out of the pitch. He was barely visible in the downpour. Greg and I had to yell at each other to be heard. The curious brown rock at the belay revealed itself as the base of a waterfall. Above, the huge "Fat City" dihedral was draining much of its runoff directly onto us. Mud, dirt, and finally, small rocks were mixed in with the frigid water. To warm up, I managed to haul a third of the way. Hammer blows indicated that Jeff was still cleaning pins. Urgency overwhelmed me.

"Just leave the damn pins!" I screamed.

"Whaaa ..."

"I said, just leave the pins ... get up here!"

Jeff picked up speed, and finally emerged through the rain, a phantom in blue.

"I hope you're getting some pictures of this!" he yelled to Greg.

My cotton pants were stuck to my legs, and I was shivering uncontrollably. When Jeff arrived I was getting a bit fuzzy. The situation was dangerous, but at the same time ludicrous. I felt like giggling and crying.

"Here we are on the stupid stone grade looking like a couple of beatniks," I sputtered.

"This is real ... this is now ... this is a freak show baby anyhow," Jeff shouted.

I could not stop shaking. Alarm passed through my mind but I could not quite seem to figure out what was important. Dryness and warmth went to frigid cold in 10 minutes. Was that serious? Greg's fixed rope was three feet away, a profound yet silent option, a way out. The world was a slow motion dance. We were at a crossroads. I knew something vital was happening but I couldn't seem to grasp it.

"What do we do?" Jeff asked.

"I don't know."

"How do you feel?"

"I don't know."

"Make a decision!" he demanded.

I soul searched for an instant. Things were too whacky. The temptation was overwhelming.

"Let's go."

Jeff craned forward. There was concern in his eyes. He wanted to be sure.

"We go?"

"We go."

"Let's go out of here!"

Epi had quietly watched the crisis unfold. From two feet away he could not hear our words.

"What do we do?" he asked.

"Let's go!"

"Whaaat?"

"Lets get the heck out of here!"

Jeff offered me his jacket. I refused. "Take it," he said. "I'm wet already." He gave me no choice, and I took his jacket gratefully. The rainshell was prewarmed and smelled like days of toil. Under the shell Jeff was wearing only a dry T-shirt. The shirt, powder blue, soon turned a wet indigo.

Greg was ahead of me furiously humping up the chord. The lower out sent me straight into the heart of our waterfall. I sensed that Greg was well above from the rhythm on the rope. Against common sense, I glanced up to check his progress. A violent firehose of water caught me in the face. An absurd story about domestic turkeys flitted through my brain. When left in the rain they have been known to drown through sheer curiosity. They gaze up in the sky, mouths agape, until they fill with water.

The mad dash to the summit was frightening. The water was pushing us around. We ascended as fast as we could, with our heads bent over for protection. Our arms and hands cramped with strain. I wished for a helmet. I feared the water-driven debris would cut the rope. Our frozen hands fumbled to switch jumars while passing knots, all without the luxury of back tying. Hanging from a single jumar 2000 feet off the deck was creepy. Six hundred feet of rope separated us from the summit.

"Oh, Lord, if it is your will that I die now, then so be it," I prayed. "But I don't know if I'm psyched to go this way."

My heart pounded furiously. I muttered my prayers over and over. Prayer lent a certain cadence to my efforts and calmed me. I looked down and saw small cascades streaming off my legs, elbows, and jacket. Far below, Jeff was still at the belay, and it looked like he was frantically trying to haul the bags. As I moved up, Jeff faded into the torrent.

It took 30 minutes to get to the summit, where Epi and I waited a distressing 15 minutes for Jeff's arrival. After days of wall living, level ground was very disorienting. Our feelings of disappointment were still veiled by a profound sense of release. I felt like a felon unexpectedly released from prison.

We had to keep moving to stay warm. The rain pounded us as we hiked down the East Ledges, and I was haunted by a sense of unreality. Having obtained an early release, we began to ponder our "retreat." We had cheated and had been cheated. I felt guilty for not wearing my rain jacket, for freezing, for making the decision to jug out.

We could never truly climb *Sunkist*. The mystery was gone, the attraction lost. Even when granted an undeserved reprieve, the fickle human soul is quick to forget the gift of deliverance. We trudged down the familiar descent in silence.

Several hours later, the three of us were in the Degnan's Loft Restaurant. I marveled at how food was brought out in such quantity. All you had to do was sit there. Jeff and I shared a toast. I could feel the cheery glow of warmth returning. The world shimmered.

Friends approached. We deflected questions with vacant stares. Fellow climbers were baffled by our miraculous re-emergence into the horizontal world.

My buddy Steve Rathbun was downstairs telling the locals how the *Sunkist* team was swallowed by the storm. He had been watching us all day.

"They're hurtin' way bad," he said. "Those guys are in the middle of a vertical river. They're in for a grim night."

Speculation, patronizing advice, half-real concern, and vicarious commentary flowed until someone interrupted. "They're not hurtin.' They're upstairs in the Loft Bar."

Notoriety in the midst of failure. People were zipping around the restaurant at a frantic pace, their words a slurry of incoherent noises. Our acquaintances wanted the full story. Some seemed obsessed with minutia, while some demanded a narrative they cared nothing about. We were the center of unwanted attention, and everything started to seem crazy. I was reduced to gazing at my interrogators with an idiotic grin.

I wished I were high on El Cap again. I was distorted, and things were happening way too fast. Then It hit me. My head fell into my swollen hands and prayer rose from my heart. I prayed for my friends. I prayed in thanks. No one noticed my rapture.

The process of climbing El Cap was no different than before. The work, the fear, the smells and sounds were all too familiar. But the internal process had changed. I realized, in retrospect, that I need not run away anymore. El Cap is no longer a big Disneyland where I could lose myself for days on end. Escape was no longer necessary. God had freed me to do what needed to be done. My puny efforts to play a deluded game were over, and no more will I attempt to justify climbing. By the grace of God I shall continue upward, free of my burden.

Postscript: One week later the three of us returned to *Sunkist*, to rappel and clean up our mess. Out of curiosity, Jeff and I led the next two classic pitches, both about A3+. Humping out the 350 pounds of rope and gear was another story.

First published in Climbing *No. 136, March 1993.*

The Triple Crown
Yosemite's real challenge

Anyone can climb when they go to Yosemite. Most people we know go for that very reason. How many of you have driven in Yosemite? I mean really driven. No. I don't mean tour driving, pulling into camp, or shuttling off to the crag. I'm talking about sport driving.

The Yosemite Valley is a wonderland so vast, that the intrepid climber could spend years exploring its steep walls of endless granite, splitter cracks, and slick boulders. For the auto or bus bound visitor, Yosemite tourist season means choking heat, rush hour traffic jams, and Big Apple parking trauma. The two activities are a world apart. Seldom do the domains brush each other. One example: tour busses stop in El Cap Meadow so the hordes can rubberneck and simultaneously snap off a few rounds of film. On the other end: the tired climber curses maddening tourist traffic on his way back from a day at the Cookie.

Some world's do collide. They did for me one dreary gray winter while living in Yosemite. As a true local, I sometimes spent periods as long as nine months without even setting foot outside the Valley. A shopping trip to Fresno was like a journey overseas, exotic and laced with an unsettling dismay at strange and unaccustomed surroundings. Boredom breeds sloth and indolence. In certain rare transcendent moments, a burst of brilliance can emerge from the listless doldroms of off-season Yosemite. One such moment came in a collaborative flash of insight one evening in the Mountain Room Bar. We invented Yosemite's Triple Crown, an event, or series of goals combining a climber's sense of intrepid exploratory adventure, with the miles of paved, stringently regulated and as yet un-exploited asphalt surface.

I figured that The Triple Crown of Yosemite driving should involve stretches of motor travel conquering the classic (and illegal) paved passages of the Valley floor. The first of the series would be the Swinging Bridge footpath. This paved trail links the one way loop near Sentinel Rock, crossing a narrow footbridge over the Merced, and eventually winding past the tent cabins into the Yosemite Lodge. I suppose it would have been the equivalent of a runout one pitch route

The second obvious line was the two mile footpath to Mirror Lake. This winding and scenic path was the realm of pedestrians, rental cyclists, and diesel belching shuttle busses. Back then, it terminated at Mirror Lake, a soon to be silted over pool. These days, it has all the aesthetic appeal of a swamp. Half Dome towers above like a broad tombstone. This very vantage, with its paved access, makes Half Dome one of the most photographed pieces of rock in the world.

The third segment of the illegal trifecta involved the one way loop running from Camp 4 down valley to the Merced river crossing at the Pohono Bridge. From Pohono Bridge the one way continued up valley to the Sentinel Bridge. This winding two lane is the traditional scene of mid summer bottlenecks and off season road races among valley locals. I must shamefully admit to wrapping my Honda around a tree on a particularly treacherous night— but that's another story. This long loop was to be the crown jewel of the coveted Triple Crown. At 12 miles it was the El Cap of illegal Valley driving— that is, if it was driven backwards.

Lead by example. One night I did the Swinging Bridge. I drove at night, cautiously edged up the bridge steps, over and through twists and dark turns into the Lodge parking lot. Mortimer, a local renowned for his extreme climbing and off-the-rock pranks, had performed the feat in months prior. His first traverse reduced the

Swinging Bridge drive from cutting edge performance to a mere a rite of passage.

Next came the Mirror Lake loop. To maintain a sportsman-like flavor, I decided on a broad daylight surgical strike. the pedestrians and cyclists posed no problem— just drive slow, smile, wave, and pretend you are on official business. the Shuttle busses were a problem. The bus drivers were well aware of current driving prohibitions. They were also armed with dispatch radios. Their Achilles heel was the fact that they were bound by schedule. Barring mishap or accident, the busses ran every fifteen minutes.

So I and a gullible friend waited at the entrance of the restricted zone. A bus lumbered by at a low speed growl. We waited seven minutes and drove, matching the speed of the shuttle. In theory our position was equidistant between the shuttle in front and the one behind. We drove, enjoying the diffused sunlight filtered through the tall oaks which lined our avenue. Later we enjoyed an afterglow similar to completing a difficult multi-pitch route— technical and a bit more committing than the Swinging Bridge.

The concept of finishing The Triple Crown rattled like an obscure skeleton in the back of my head. Driving the Loop backwards— I treated it like a rock climb I wanted very badly but couldn't quite screw up the nerve to complete. "It'll always be there..." I thought. We contemplated posting lookouts with walkie talkies, doing it during a freak park closure or properly disguising ourselves as tourists ignorant enough to not know better. Either the logistics were too cumbersome or the plans nullified the challenge to the point of zero risk. and then what would the point be?

I subconsciously contrived lesser challenges in vain attempt to forget the real issue. One night I drove through the employee housing in the Annex, weaving round barbecue pits and crumping over gutters. "Bah. Nothing but a boulder problem," my car mate said with contempt. All the extra credit in the world doesn't add up to one shred of the true test. I figured the annex drive/boulder problem was like doing a sit down start to an El Cap route.

I contemplated the Chapel Bridge path parallel to the Swinging Bridge. The structure which spans the Merced had a narrow width. We measured the distance between the guardrails. We then measured the width of my Honda Civic. I had three inches of clearance on each side. Then I wrecked my Honda. I was on Loop and driving the legal (for my purposes the wrong) direction.

I recently heard that the infamous Mortimer borrowed a car from a pretty young ladies and became the first to drive across the Chapel Bridge. Another un-substantiated (but most likely true) rumor is that Tucker Tech and the late great Dave Gadd drove a Ford Bronco to the Lower Falls Bridge got out and took a leak. There have also been rumors of valet cars from the Awahnee being driven up the Mirror Lake Loop., The reportedly best performers were Hum-vees. Again, all hearsay

The three things I regret having never completed in Yosemite was the Thriller, Astroman and the final jewel of the Triple Crown. The Thriller and Astroman are almost regular events, but I haven't heard of anyone doing the Loop backwards. If you've done, it let us know. If we don't hear from you, then we can assume that the gauntlet is there. All it takes is for someone to be pick it up.

Previously unpublished.

The Lifer,
Tucker Tech, the archetypal climbing bum

Tucker Tech sat in Yosemite's Mountain Room Bar, stewing. His love life was in shambles and the weather was grim this winter night in 1989. His status on the Yosemite Search and Rescue Team was becoming increasingly tenuous. The only consolation was a huge pitcher of "Old English Light," a rude hybrid of cheap vodka and draft beer. Every so often a perplexed cocktail waitress would pass, noting that Tucker, a regular patron, was getting drunker without reducing the level of beer in the pitcher. The brew's gold hue became lighter and lighter as more vodka was added to the mix. On stage, a country western band was playing homogenized hits, tailored to neither offend nor particularly entertain. At the lead singer's feet sat a huge tumbleweed, the band's mascot. After a short intermission the band resumed and Tucker, in a fit of righteous pique, began braying, "Go kill yourselves!" His pleas were ignored. Tucker strode up to the stage, grabbed the tumbleweed, walked over to the fireplace, and dumped it in the blaze. He then returned to his table, sat down primly, and, under the appalled stare of the other patrons, sipped his drink and smacked his lips. Another night in the life of Tucker Tech.

Tucker Tech is gnarly, and painfully authentic. Many climbers yearn to live the consummate climbing-bum lifestyle. Few do it. As Eric Beck, the archetypal climbing bum of the 1960s, once said, "At either end of the social spectrum there lies a leisure class." Tucker is one of the few in this "leisure class," who have stuck it out for so long. He has no job other than rare or seasonal part-time work. During the summer months he spends a few weeknight hours collecting tickets for the Yosemite Theater's John Muir show. Camming-unit repairs, copperhead sales, and the rare poker game fill out the long months between work. He files no income tax and keeps no physical address. He hasn't for the last 17 years. Such transience engenders a great deal of freedom and relaxation, but is also bereft of the physical and psychological comforts that most people depend on. There is no doctor, dentist, or retirement plan in Tucker's future. There have been many seasons of no money, no food, and no beer. Loneliness becomes an enduring mistress; flesh-and-blood sweethearts are not attracted by poverty. On the other hand, Tucker has no bills, obligations, or schedule, save for the changing of the seasons.

Eric Brand, a noted Bay Area climber and longtime friend, says, "Tucker is sort of a throwback to the old days, where climbing was more of a committed way of life than a hip weekend pursuit." Dan McDevitt, a Valley local, guide, and Tucker's frequent climbing partner, says, "Tucker has always done his own thing and has never complained about it. How many of us can live that way and be totally content?"

In climbing, Tucker maintains that he is "delving into mediocrity," but an impressive track record belies his self-deprecation. In his 17 years of climbing he has amassed an enviable tick list, with 32 El Cap ascents, including well-known classics and such forgotten lines as *Pacemaker, Lost World,* and *Realm of the Flying Monkeys,* as well as extended high-tech outings like *Aurora.* He also has done numerous early (and sometimes solo) repeats of Grade Vs and VIs on other Valley walls — a solo of *Tenaya's Terror* (A4) on Mount Watkins in 1990 and the second ascent of *Rainbow* on the Falls Wall in the early 1980s represent the tip of an iceberg of experience. During the last 10 years Tech has established over 170 new routes in Yosemite Valley, ranging from high-quality multi-climbs up to 5.11+. As of last fall he had climbed

1000 routes in Joshua Tree. On his best days Tucker leads 5.11+ cracks and 5.12a face, and solos up to 5.10.

Tech started climbing in 1977 at the age of 21. His initial forays took him to many outcrops in California's Bay Area near his home in Marin County, then extended to Lovers Leap and Yosemite Valley. While attending the College of Marin, Tucker became an assistant instructor for the mountaineering program, and soon got interested in longer routes. He also began shaping a trademark stoicism that would see him through the bleakest circumstances Early failures on several big routes did nothing to curb Tucker's doggedness. Eric Brand, who has taken Yosemite-style big-wall climbing to Greenland and the Himalaya, was one of Tech's early partners.

"Tucker took me out on my very first day of climbing. From the outset he struck me as competent and solid. We got along quite well and as our skills increased, so did our aspirations. We were both psyched to climb bigger and bigger things. One of the first major routes we tried together was the Leaning Tower *West Face.* We had to retreat." Next the pair attempted the *West Buttress,* an awkward, grassy Grade VI on the left side of El Cap. They bailed in bad weather 13 pitches up. Undeterred, they made a serious go at an even more ambitious objective, the *Dawn Wall* to the right of the *Nose.* Again, bunk weather. Brand continues, "These failures did nothing to dissuade me and certainly not Tucker. If anything, these early attempts and subsequent successes tempered each of us. We learned how to be patient, how to accept defeat, and also how to value success."

John Tucker Tech was born on January 15, 1958, in Marin County. He goes by Tucker to avoid a reference to his absentee biological father, John. His only living blood relative is his brother Steve Tech, 38, whom Tucker terms, "definitely the better half of the family." The same high regard does not apply to the rest of the Techs. Tucker recalls, "From all accounts, my biological father was a drug dealer. He seemed to hold an ability inherent to the modern sport climber — he could move about with no visible means of support."

Affirms Steve Tech, "Our biological father used to drive around in brand-new cars while our mother lived in poverty. He split when Tucker was born. He never even went to see him."

Their mother remarried and then, two years after Tucker's birth, died of an aneurysm, leaving young Tucker and Steve in the custody of their stepfather. Their only blood relative was an infant, conceived by their mother and stepfather, who died of SIDS.

Tucker remarks, "We had an awesomely dysfunctional family. I was raised by a stepfather who hit me with all the angst of having me as a stepson. He was the epitome of all I despised." Tucker was, and is, bullheaded to a tee.

The brothers became further removed from the household when their stepfather remarried.

"She came along and made it hell on both of us, but especially for Tucker," Steve says. "He refused to change his ways, which by this time was taking on, you know, the climber's lifestyle." Their stepfather died of cancer in 1987.

"It was a slow and painful death," says Tucker. "It is rather disturbing watching a control freak die slowly." The entire inheritance went to their stepmother.

Tucker abandoned college in the early 1980s, and soon found himself passing most of his time in Yosemite, either out-of-bounds camping or staying in the Camp 4 Search and Rescue Site. In Yosemite he found enough suffering to kill what he called, "the pain of this disease called life." He did a six-month stint in Boulder, taking in the Colorado scene, whiling away most of his time on, "twisted road trips which had more to do with mind expansion than serious climbing." In 1981, following a storm-plagued trip to Chamonix and the Dolomites, Tucker and two friends, Everett Gordon and his wife, Maggie, took off on a ski traverse of Denali. They experienced minus 40 and 50 degree temperatures and were successful in traversing the mountain, yet failed to reach the actual summit. At one point one of the Gordons slipped, dragging Tucker on an uncontrolled 300-foot slide. The rope that joined them snared a protruding rock, averting disaster. This trip spelled the end of Tucker's big alpine aspirations.

The Valley drew him back and, if nothing else, Tech's venture into alpine climbing toughened his approach to rock climbing. He forsook the usual necessities like harnesses, opting instead for a swami belt, which he still wears. The plush sit harness I once game him ended up for sale on the Camp 4 bulletin board. "The less comfortable you are, the less you are apt to hang around (while) aid climbing," he explains. "It will keep you from festering around in your lower steps." Tucker also swore off other amenities such as tape for crack climbing and gloves or knee pads for walls. Another odd move was his habit of wearing sandals year round; he could often be seen in the Valley plodding through snow in Birkenstocks, sans socks.

Dan McDevitt, who has done 10 winter walls, witnessed the benefits of such deprivation on an early 1980s ascent of El Cap's *Mescalito.*

"Tucker is probably the most oblivious man to pain since Hercules. The guy never complains. On *Mescalito* he dropped his sleeping bag from 800 feet up. I guess I had a mean look on my face ëcause Tucker quickly said that we weren't going to bail. For six days he'd sleep huddled in the fetal position and wake up covered with snow. Worst cold I've ever felt on a wall. Not a single word of complaint."

Alex Hinton, a guiding client of mine from L.A., and I circle a rain-swept Hidden Valley Campground in Joshua Tree searching for Tech for interviewing. We finally catch up with him in Yucca Valley. He is at a friend's house waiting for a break in the weather. To me, his host, a young lady, appears relieved when we take him off her hands, though Alex thinks she is unhappy about losing Tucker to us. Either way, Tucker is oblivious. He is pleased that I have gone through such a great deal of trouble just to talk to him. We retreat to a Motel 6 as darkness falls.

Our meeting is a great excuse for Tech to vent his seething passions. Anyone who knows him can vouch for his acidic wit, grueling monologues, and destructive antics. My mind wanders. In my imagination I see the room in flames with a stark naked, bottle-wielding Tucker Tech dancing a snappy jig in the parking lot. Alex settles down facing Tucker. I idly flick the TV remote control. Tucker's sharp rebuke snaps me back. "Don't do that. Mindless viewing is not my forte. It opens a Pandora's Box of base ideas.

As I start asking questions, Tech's grin threatens to split his face. He has a captive audience and knows it. I've known Tucker for years and have taken the liberty to provide him with his favorite brew, Elephant Malt. Tech is the same as ever. His thirst for intriguing discussion and strong liquor is unabated. His thinning hair is longer than ever. His face is ruddy from the desert wind, the peeling red nose finding a sympathetic background against his cheeks, which are in need of a shave. His particularly unkempt appearance and tightly furrowed brow adds to a demeanor that is more sinister than ever. He is skinnier than I remember. He smokes intently, vigorously exercising a habit he used to deride. Tucker downs an immense slug of beer and smiles, saying "Ah, the bread of my affliction." He pauses, his brow knit, and scrutinizes my face, searching for reaction. "You know, Pete, this is as near as I will ever get to heaven." I gaze about the drab, impersonal room and release a weary sigh.

Tech's build does not lend itself to the sinewy pursuits of the modern rock climber. He is stout, a low-slung five-foot-nine firmly anchored to the earth. Several years ago in the Valley some friends of mine began slandering Tech, whose physique did not match their ideals. "He's as strong as an ox," I said. The immediate reply was a sneering, "Well, we should hitch him up to a cart." This off-the-cuff remark caught a truth that perhaps was not intended. Tech's strength has enabled him to jump on his bike in Marin County and ride to Joshua Tree via Yosemite, a distance of 550 miles, in seven stormy days. Or solo four El Cap routes in five weeks wearing a swami belt and cleaning pitches with the haul bag on his back.

Steve Tech describes how Tucker has been helping him build a house in Yosemite West, a private enclave located inside park boundaries. "We can't afford to rent heavy equipment so we have to do everything by hand. We're out there clearing land, digging stumps, chopping wood, and all that kind of thing. Chips, salsa, beer, and pizza are all he needs. He does an incredible job. I'd pit Tucker against a backhoe any day."

The brothers both have the same stocky Tech build. Crack a good joke and both will flash a Cheshire-cat grin. Both are intelligent, though Steve claims that Tucker always had an easier time in school. Tucker exhibits an otherwise rare degree of deference and consideration in the presence of Steve.

At 19, Tucker invested the Social Security check from his mother's death into a hobby that had been only a fantasy due to poverty, dropping the entire $2000 into a coin collection. He based his selection partly on personal research and partly on intuition. "I was young and had some time on my hands. My specific choices were based on a general idea of what was going up. All of a sudden I had $20,000 out of my initial investment." His investment ultimately financed several years of "high" living. Right up through the month his money ran out, Tucker still drank his quota of import beer, never considering a cheaper brand.

His budding interest in detail, exercised through coin collecting, fully bloomed when applied to climbing. A morning visit to the Yosemite Lodge Cafeteria will more often than not find Tucker scrupulously writing about and sketching obscure Valley nooks and crannies. The Yosemite guidebook author Don Reid has been in a unique position to appreciate and benefit from Tucker's inquiring mind. The preface to the new edition of Yosemite Climbs: Free Climbs contains the dedication: "Special thanks to Tucker Tech for sharing his extensive log of new and corrected route information."

Reid notes, "Tucker and I definitely share a kind of kinship of the forgotten and little-known crags. For example, Tucker is the only guy I know of who has actually done the *Salami Ledge* route on the West Face of El Cap."

Tech's interest in minutia is reflected in his lust to claim new ground. From Parkline Slab above El Portal below the Valley's west entrance to the southwest face of Half Dome, he's left few spots untouched. *Free Climbs* lists his name on nearly 150 first ascents.

Several local climbers have derided a few of Tucker's routes as mere stretches of defaced rock, dead vegetation, and meaningless lines of bolts. Some of his first are certainly classics, others certainly not. Regardless, Tech is unfazed, and will waste no time in comparing "my own minute efforts to impose my will on my surroundings," to what he calls "the colossal efforts of the National Park Service to destroy wilderness in the United States." He says ardently, "If you want to see the impact that climbing has had on Yosemite go to Glacier Point and look over the edge." You'll see the swimming pools, restaurants, asphalt roads, and hear the roar of trucks, busses, and autos thousands of feet below. Any trace of climbing gear or climbers is absent.

The route names Tucker chooses are often puns, reflective of his general irreverence. *Roadside Attraction* resides next to *Roadside Infraction,* while uphill lies Tucker's *Roadside Destruction.* The common themes revolve around alcohol, sex, and nihilism. Many names are obscene, and lash out at the unsuspecting reader. Foaming at the Crotch and Gerbil Launcher are some examples of his humor.

In the motel room, Tucker has filled one of the ashtrays with dead butts and run out of cigarettes. We walk 50 yards to a convenience store, a bastion of light and bustle. Behind the counter are the owners, two swarthy Middle Eastern brothers absorbed by the television, which bathes their faces in a flashing blue radiance. The Republicans have swept the elections and through the static the commentator rages about an impending G.O.P. landslide.

"G.O.P., G.O.P. — what is this G.O.P.?" the brothers ask, concerned about this powerful, vaguely menacing entity, which has thrust itself upon them with no warning. Their eyes light upon Tucker, who stands scowling at the television with an air of informed contempt. They ask Tucker, "G.O.P., what is this G.O.P., do you know?"

Tucker replies with an icy stare, "The whole thing you are watching is a mere piece of fiction. It is an elaborate and clever joke. The initials G.O.P. stand for Grim Old Parody. You need not be concerned."

The brothers turn to each other with quizzical expressions. Tucker and I turn and walk out the glass door into the darkness.

Back in our room, I ask Tucker about an accident he had in the summer of 1989. He was scoping new routes around the base of Elephant Rock, soloing 4th and easy 5th-class terrain, dressed in his usual Birkenstocks and ratty shorts. My query invites Tucker to embark on one of his favorite themes, death. He dramatically vents a huge cloud of smoke as if to punctuate the story. His head tilts back, eyes narrowing as both hands rise in slow pantomime. Alex is engrossed.

"As I started down climbing a steep step near the *Straight Error* route I grabbed a 40-foot-high detached pillar of rock. The thing must have weighed 20 tons. It's one of those things you'd never dream of moving."

Here Tucker pauses and twists his lips into a sneer.

"The block swung loose and began smashing me. At the same time I was spit off and fell 50 feet to the base of the step."

Tucker lay unconscious for several hours. He came to and muddle about and realized he was not dead. Next, he hiked up the several hundred feet of 3rd and 4th-class slabs to where his bike was stashed. Then he rode to the public showers at Yosemite Lodge.

"I looked in the mirror and saw I was a terrible mess. I was unrecognizable from all the clotted blood."

Tucker raises his Elephant Malt and takes a belt. He is taking a perverse pleasure in detailing his experience. He lifts a swatch of greasy hair and points to a crease in his right ear.

"This ear was halfway ripped off. I pressed it back into place and continued washing up. At this point a Curry Company employee saw me and freaked. He began insisting that I need an ambulance. I told him to piss off. The poor bastard thought I was crazy and ran off to tell his manager that someone was dying in the shower room ..."

Tucker can barely restrain his laughter. His head sways to and fro. His mouth chews the air like a giraffe grazing the top of a tree, savoring that which is beyond the grasp of lesser creatures. His whole body shakes with laughter.

"... and then I went to work at the Muir Show," Tucker continues. "My boss was not very happy with the way I looked."

After collecting tickets for several hours he went to the Mountain Room Bar to treat his condition with alcohol.

"Everybody was buying me drinks. All my friends were hoping that I would pass out so they could take me to the clinic. Several days later an M.D. friend sized me up in an informal examination in the parking lot. His assessment of my condition was four cracked ribs and a possible ruptured pleural cavity. He told me to go to the hospital." Tucker's eyes sparkle with mirth. "I told him that the only medicine I need, I can get at the Deli."

Then Tech's brow knits. His eyes narrow and bore into my own with cold precision.

"The truth is, Pete, you're going to die and I'm going to die." He glares at me then turns to wink at Alex as if sharing an inside joke. "Some of us have embraced new ideals, but cannot escape old realities."

I recall a similar story. In 1990, soloing at the base of Washington Column, Tech was poised on several munge hummocks when the whole mess cut loose. He fell 40 feet.

"I fell and broke my nose and banged myself up considerably. ... I ripped the tissue between my nasal cavity and upper lip and my lower lip was smashed through my upper teeth. For a while I could close my mouth and blow blood bubbles out my mouth through my nose."

Again Tech refused to seek medical aid. He couldn't afford it, and declared, "Doctors don't know anything anyway."

I also recall that as a veteran member of the Yosemite Search and Rescue Team (YOSAR), Tech has often faced the grim task of recovering bodies in various states of decay and disintegration. He shares with some other YOSAR members a rather unwholesome sense of humor and preoccupation with death. Sitting on the motel bed watching the man indulge his morbid side I'm reminded of another Tucker story. One day by the Merced River, Tucker launched into one of his spasms of near despair. Words like "death" and "suicide" popped up with annoying frequency. He was sitting by the river with Steve Ortner, a fellow YOSAR member. Ortner was somewhere between six and a half and seven feet tall. He was also proportionately strong. Tucker began again, "I wish I was dead ..."

Steve abruptly turned, grabbed Tucker, and shoved his head under the water. Tucker thrashed about unable to break the steely grip. After an interminable minute Steve relented and resurrected a gasping Tucker.

"Do you still want to kill yourself?"

"No," Tucker choked between wheezes.

"Then shut up."

Tucker's relationships with women have played a pivotal role in his life. The Yosemite social scene is notorious for its complex webs of sexual politics. Strong partnerships and friendships have been sundered by sexual intrigue, and Tucker has not been spared from the darker times. He has a soft spot reserved for the fairer sex and has consequently paid the price. In the mid-1980s, a year-and-a-half relationship came to a messy end. A love triangle soon multiplied geometrically. Tucker fell "full force" and retreated to El Cap to "crush out the pain of living. I wanted to destroy every last grain of emotion. I wanted nothing more than to feel nothing." The result was his four El Cap route solo binge, a landmark in his climbing career ñ which seemed to change nothing. When his friend Jeff Perrin commented in regard to women, "Nice guys finish last," Tucker snapped back, "Nice guys get mean!"

"In the past I've seen him take a woman who wronged him and publicly rake her over the coals, just as brutal and unrelenting as can be," says Steve Tech. "Today he mostly walks away from such a situation and tries to be alone. When he gets bummed out he withdraws and listens to his music." Tucker now travels and climbs with many different women. When asked if there is anyone special, he'll give you an answer like, "Women come and women go. The less I seem to care, the more things seem to happen."

Besides his brother and girlfriends, Tucker's only other serious relationship has been a long association with the National Park Service. Last year, Tucker's career with YOSAR, which spanned over a decade, came to an end when he was expelled from the team. Evidently, his years of frank and unrestrained criticism of the Park Service and other governmental entities had not sat well with the authorities. Tech claims that the NPS's environmental and legal abuses "would fill a good-sized novel." He declines to divulge specifics. John Dill, head of YOSAR, declined to comment on Tucker's departure other than, "Tucker is a good guy and a good worker ... however, we need more participatory members on the site. If there was a big emergency, I would still put him to work in a heartbeat."

With his YOSAR service at an end, Tech looks forward to more travel and climbing. He also plans on spending time with his brother. "I'm assuming he will retire up on the hill (Yosemite West) with me," Steve says. "He will always have a place in my house ..."

Tucker is not to be trifled with. His keen rhetorical skills work in concert with remorseless will, and he has reduced many to tears. While Tucker's verbal blade can inflict pain, it also hacks through pretense.

Eric Brand says, "Tucker smells people like a shark smells a bleeding swimmer. If he senses any form of insincerity he will not hesitate to go for the throat. He is loyal, honest, and a good friend. If he sees you lying or not being true to yourself he will call you on it. He is not one to coddle you with any bullshit. At the same time, you know that when he gives you a compliment, even a little scrap, it means a lot."

Dan McDevitt adds, "The thing about Tucker is there is no hob-nobbing around. He'll tell you right to your face what he thinks about you and what you are saying. I'd say that's one of his greatest attributes. I can also see how that would piss some people off."

Even Tech observes, "I alienate more people than who like me. It's surprising that sometimes I don't get beat up."

Tech applies this sense of honesty to his life. He does not steal or lie, even under great pressure. He will joke and fib during chit cat, but if the talk is serious he will bore straight ahead. I have seen Tucker go hungry and lose weight during lean times. Never have I heard him solicit aid, contemplate thievery, or complain. Despite his pride, there are times Tech will apologize.

In 1990, Tech, Jeff Perrin, and I were climbing *Pacemaker,* an A4 route on El Capitan. We were four days into the climb after having weathered several days of snow and falling ice. On the fourth night, Tech polished off his dinner, a rude assortment of kippered herring, a few stale crackers, and close to a pint of vodka. It was a rough night and about 2 a.m., he began heaving. I was stuck directly below him on a very small sloping ledge.

"Tucker, you're puking on me!"

Between heaves, Tucker responded, "I am not hitting you. It is falling clear of you."

The next wave struck me square on the hood. My only recourse was to burrow deeper into my bivy sack. The next morning I waved the odious evidence in Tucker's face. To my astonishment he apologized profusely. I felt sheepish. A heartfelt apology from Tucker was something I had never heard, nor have I since.

Several days later, we were back on terra firma and on one particularly intense night, the beer flowed freely and emotions ran high. Tucker broke out of his shell and openly expressed his kinship with us as partners and close friends.

"I love you guys," he said. "Sometimes I don't think I deserve friendships like this." Jeff and I were surprised and touched by his sincerity. The next day I strode up to Tucker with a smile on my face.

He stopped me cold with a scowl. "By the way, Pete, I cannot be held accountable for anything I said last night.

First published in Climbing *No 153, June, 1995.*

Midnight Lightning
The myth and magic of America's most famous boulder problem

There was something about the Hendrix name, the location, and all the history surrounding it that kept me psyched. I was on it practically every morning before going cragging — that was for seven months," says Kurt Smith, whose nickname slowly evolved from "the Kid" to "the General," as his climbing feats grew.

"I eventually got to the mantel, fell off a few times, and took a rest day. Then I got the two biggest guys I knew — Tracy Dorton and Troy Johnson — to spot me. I guess people heard I was close because, I shit you not, there were about 50 people there waiting for me to get on it at 10 a.m.. I went up, did it, and everyone went crazy! They were cheering. I was yelling. I took everyone to the Deli and we were gurgled by noon. Sending the Lightning was probably the highest moment in my life."

[Kurt Smith describing his fourth ascent of Midnight Lightning.]

"Ziss is more than chust a problem. It is a feeling, a legend, a story," says the man. He squats in the dust poking a stick through powder-dry crust into hard ground. Brows pinched in concentration he digs for words. "It is ..." He pauses for a moment. Then his head snaps up. "It is a dream!"

Kurt Albert, of Germany, knows about climbing dreams — he has lived his share from Europe to Patagonia, the Himalaya to the Antarctic. We sit, crouched in the shadow of the Big Columbia Boulder at the center of Yosemite Valley's Camp 4. The dream arcs above, a hovering mystery set in stone. It is the boulder problem *Midnight Lightning*.

A trick of fate brought the *Lightning* to the center of American climbing lore. A very long time ago, a huge granite monolith tore from its moorings high above the valley, crashed down the talus, and bullied its way through the forest. The titanic multi-faceted lump came to rest on the flood plain that is now Camp 4. Here the Big Columbia Boulder became a reference point, an icon, at the dawn of Valley climbing. As soon as climbers arrived they began establishing standard-setting boulder problems on its flanks. The *Steck Overhang* of the 1950s and the *Chouinard Overhang,* the *Robbins Eliminate,* and *Bates' Problem* of the 1960s, each set the hurdle of Valley bouldering one notch higher.

According to legend, *Midnight Lightning* began as a dream in the late John "Yabo" Yablonski's LSD-enhanced mind. The moniker was borrowed from a deep, bluesy Hendrix track.

"Yabo was out on this weird trip one day," recalls John Bachar. "He was f...in' around spacing out on rocks and shit all day long. I just got in from climbing and Yabo runs up to me and Ron Kauk and says, 'Hey, Bachar, you gotta check this out, man!'"

The trio walked over to the Big Columbia where Yabo, with pupils glazed and dilated, pointed up at a series of supposed holds — square-cut sidepulls following the only weakness on the boulder's east face. "Me and Kauk look at each other. Yabo's making a pantomime gesture telling us there's a route up there. It's totally silly! By this time Kauk and I are rolling with laughter. We keep tellin' him, 'Yer f...in' nuts Yabo. What are you going to do at that roof? There are no holds up there!'"

At 10 feet, a blank wave-like roof looms out to the right, over-hanging the base of the climb by several feet. At its lip, this over-hang turns abruptly into an easy angled slab. The first crux of *Midnight Lightning* links the lower sidepulls to the lip of the roof using the only available hold: a double incut, shaped like a horizontal lightning bolt.

A few days after his vision, Yabo tried the moves. Before long Bachar and Kauk had joined in and fallen under the spell. "We basically worked on the problem every other day for nearly a year. It took forever to get the lightning-bolt hold and forever to match it," recalls Bachar. "Then came the big problem — turning the lip. We'd come off again and again, and come down on this slab below. That was a real heel shaker. Before anyone ever dreamed of bouldering pads."

The key to the first moves, as they discovered, is to grab the right edge of the lightning-bolt hold with the right hand. The move is big and powerful. Taller climbers can make the span and also match hands with one or both feet planted on decent edges. Shorter folk find various degrees of airborne tricks necessary: from deadpoints with feet pasted to dime-edges to feet-off dynos.

At the lip, tall climbers find their equalizer in the perilous foot-to-hand rockover. This move has scored countless nasty bumps and heel bruises, several broken wrists, and even a few injured spotters.

One fateful day in the spring of 1978 a crowd gathered in camp to watch Kauk and Bachar trying the insurmountable problem. Kauk's feet swung out as both hands clenched by the tips of his fingers onto the lightning-bolt hold. Jim Bridwell, who considered himself the king of Valley climbing back then, happened to walk by just as Kauk moved strongly to the lip.

"Bridwell watches and says, 'No way. What's this?'" Bachar recalls.

Kauk got his foot up and did the impossible-looking move, stretching for the distant incut that lies three feet back from the boulder's lip. No one knew what was up ahead, but after digging through moss to find holds on the slab, Kauk was soon jumping up and down on top of the boulder.

Bachar laughs, remembering Bridwell's baffled response: "He walked off and all he said was, 'Cool.' He didn't even know what he'd seen."

My own affair with *Midnight Lightning* began when I was a boulderer in backwater Boise, Idaho. It was the beginning of the

1980s. I had only been climbing for two or three years when I heard of this horrendous problem in Yosemite with "the hardest moves in the world." A short while later my friends and I saw a photo of the legendary climb in *Mountain* magazine. A shirtless, ripped powerhouse was crazily extended on square-cut edges. Below his feet was the cryptic lightning bolt, an outline drawn on the rock's surface in chalk. To us, Yosemite was a dreamy granite paradise — of endless walls, epic megaclimbs, and real-life super-heroes. That stark white lightning bolt drawing was the dream condensed.

I moved to Yosemite some years later. By then, Bachar had snapped off a useful horn at the lip of *Midnight Lightning,* making the problem even more difficult. Nevertheless, he had soon incorporated it into his training circuit, hucking laps, climbing it barefoot or with a weight belt. During a short visit from Colorado, Skip Guerin, one of the world's most talented — and unheralded — climbers, had become the third human to pull the lip and top out on the climb, doing so just days before Kurt Smith's long-awaited success.

Nevertheless, the halcyon days of Valley climbing were over. The area's dominance of high-end free climbing had waned. It was now hip to disparage Yosemite and its insular scene. Interviewed in an issue of *Climbing* in 1986, Kim Carigan visiting from Australia, encapsulated popular opinion: "The Valley is a little world, a very little world, with little people."

When I pulled into Camp 4 that same year, the cliffs looked mind-numbingly big. Even the boulders were big, and *Midnight Lightning* appeared just as unattainable as I'd imagined. I gazed wistfully up at the featureless rock. In my early days, the closest I came to trying the climb was curiously fondling the first polished holds.

As I stayed, the months turned into seasons and the seasons to years. And every year the brightness meter of Valley life would inevitably hit a low ebb. I found my lowest point in winter. The Valley floor turned into a soggy sponge. Water stood in puddles. Short gray days drove seasonal residents out. Girls, who'd worked temporary jobs, split back to school. I couldn't afford to travel. I was stuck, forced to remember how alone I was. Some days I'd wake up so hungover that I couldn't make a fist. The company of my bros became terminally annoying as I tired of hearing them run their stupid, ugly gobs day after day.

After a few depressing winters I hit on a solution: I would train and boulder. Around 1990 the discovery of a steep crag, Jailhouse Rock gave me and a handful of friends a good winter outlet. The wicked overhanging crag held dozens of sport climbs — an hour and a half away.

With new fitness and a positive attitude gained from sport climbing, I finally began to try *Midnight Lightning*. Like most aspirants, I eventually mastered the hand match at the lightning-bolt hold and was soon falling off the lip of the roof. The temptation to toprope the problem was great. But I figured I'd rather fail than suffer the scoffing of the "rock police." So my partners and I snuck a mattress to the *Lightning's* base. The mattress — a furry mass of leaves, spider webs, and mildew — took some of the spine compression out of our repeated falls, if only for a while. We kept it stashed under a nearby boulder until it was confiscated by the Park Service.

Out at Jailhouse Rock one cool gray day in March 1991, I warmed up and redpointed a 5.13b, physically the hardest route I had done. In the afternoon, I pulled into Camp 4, calm and replete in my post-redpoint glow, looking for nothing more than a warm-down session. The weather, the boulders, and the scenery were uniformly dull gray. Everything was still and damp.

Camp 4 was empty except for two shiftless rummies: Cade "Lazy Boy" Lloyd and Eric "Klaus" Kohl. Here they were as always, hanging around, pretending to boulder, killing time. Cade was toting a brace of standard-issue Old English 800s. Eric was sipping a sickly sweet inner-city cocktail called Brass Monkey from a garish 32-ounce bottle. It was only 3 p.m., but both were nearly hammered, approaching the perfect mental state for an evening at Degnan's Deli — bliss or hell depending on your state of mind. For weeks I hadn't been near that place.

I did a few easier problems. The pair swayed after me, hoping to latch onto some free entertainment. When I walked up to the Big Columbia Boulder they perked up.

"Whatcha gonna get on, Biggie?" Cade slurred. "Be careful, it's awful slickery today."

When I stepped up to the *Lightning,* they were overcome with childlike mirth. A great gift had dropped out of the sky to help fill the gray void between the afternoon buzz and an evening's power drinking. They placed themselves close enough to see every movement, yet far away enough to be absolved of spotting duty.

Cade had tried the problem again and again over the years, finally shrugging it off with the typical Valley local it'll-always-be-there attitude. "Biggie, you'll never send it!" he mocked.

I pulled up into the initial sidepulls and set my feet to launch for the bolt hold. I flew up and out, barely latching it: desperate. I was definitely out of sync, but clung on. Heckling from below filtered through the static of my mind: "He's out of there ..."

I re-gripped and matched on the crimp, wobbling.

"Lookin' sketchy ..."

More chuckles from below made me more determined than ever. I got both hands to the lip, just as I'd done a dozen times, just as my friends had seen again and again and watched me tumble. Still no idea how to do the mantel. Undercling right, right foot on the sloper, same as always. Beyond this point lay the unknown — a place where only living legends and heroes dared to go. The next decent hold — a door-jamb incut — was a long way away and, as always, I had no time to think. My left palm pressed flat against the smooth granite, just above the sloping mantel edge. Nothing doing.

I lost friction and my hand slid down. It stopped at the very edge of the overhang. There, I pinched the bottom of the sloper, the lip of the roof — and found the pinch yielded some unexpected security, generating mysterious leverage.

My center of gravity shifted inward and I began to rock over. I weighted my right foot, and stretched out my right arm, creeping it forward inch by inch. As my fingers curled over that doorjamb hold, I woke up as though from a dream.

"He did it," Klaus blurted in a stunned monotone, addressing no one. "He did it."

I came down shaky and elated. Grabbing Eric's nearly empty

bottle of Brass Monkey, I took a long pull. By the time we got to the Deli I'd busted into Cade's Olde E and the world was spinning like a carousel.

The next morning I woke up, my head in a cloudy haze. Sections of the preceding day assembled themselves in disjointed images: I'd done both my hardest climb and my hardest boulder problem the same afternoon. I felt a gnawing emptiness. I was sore. I walked to the cafeteria for a late coffee. There, a few rheumy-eyed friends hung out nursing their cups, looking self-satisfied. I sat down.

"So," someone said, "I heard you did the *Lightning* yesterday."

"Yeah," I answered.

Another perked in, "I heard you couldn't send at first."

"Yeah, man," someone interrupted, "I heard you drank a whole bottle of Klaus's Brass Monkey, then you finally did it."

I looked around the table at the red, expectant eyes.

"Yeah," I sighed. "That's what happened."

First published in Climbing *No. 195, June 2000.*

A Rock and a Hard Place

Hammer time on the Porcelain Wall

.

Winter 1989. I am in a dingy, cramped, and foul- smelling room in the Yosemite Lodge. Eric Kohl is expounding on hard aid climbing. He leans forward, "Charlie Fowler once said hard aid is like defusing a time bomb, which I see as a good description. I see it all as a suicide mission. It sorta manifests itself with having a screwed-up lifestyle — it and your hard aid get more addicting." "What about Life?" I ask.

"What about it? I've got no purpose. I don't know what I want. It's like that Suicidal Tendencies song *Get Whacked.* I'm up to get whacked, not have a good time."

Eric stops, sips his Old English and leans back.

"I don't know if I mean that. It's hard to explain. All I know is that these routes I put up are not a public service. They are sorta like that whole Charlie Fowler defuse-the-time-bomb bit. If people go up there they'll get what they deserve, and," he adds with a grin, "they might get whacked."

He's the one who's whacked, I think to myself. I'll never climb with this guy.

Six years later I'm with Eric on a new route on the Porcelain Wall in Yosemite. Being with him is a minor miracle. Our last

65

encounter, in 1991, involved an inebriated argument and ended with me shoving him 20 feet off Jeff Perrin's deck. A friend was shocked to learn that we were planning a wall together. "I thought you hated him." Hate? Eric may be the only person in Yosemite who has driven me to violence, but I never hated him, just saw things differently.

Climbing with Eric was my chance to see if the rumors that he had mellowed were true. Over the phone his diction certainly sounded less vitriolic, but would we end up pushing each other off the portaledges?

I had my own problems. For 10 years I had been a subsistence dweller, scraping a living, doing whatever it took to get on a climb. Now, after two years of marriage, I share a life with someone else. My time is no longer my own. Harder yet, where I live is no longer my choice. First I get dragged to Colorado where every time we settle in, Charisse makes us move. Then the clincher, she gets accepted to medschool in Des Moines. Yes, that's right, Des Moines, as in *Iowa*. A three-year sentence more painful than any big wall, and at least walls are character building and wonderfully useless.

The Porcelain Wall, a.k.a. the Diving Board, dwells in the shadow of Yosemite's Half Dome. The Porcelain's close proximity to one of the earth's most famous lumps of rock relegates this burnished-nickel wall of granite to unmerited obscurity. Before our attempt, the Porcelain Wall had been climbed only twice. The first ascent was a strange historical footnote in the life of Warren J. Harding, who we all know from his first ascent of El Cap via *The Nose* in 1958. Harding completed the Porcelain Wall in 1976 with the then neophyte wall climbers Steve Bosque and Dave Lomba. A second ascent came in June, 1987, when John Barbella and Walt Shipley established a new route, *The Luminescent Wall*, (VI 5.10 A4) on the left side of the face.

Bosque, who, like Lomba, eventually went on to leave his mark on Yosemite, recalls, "We were total rookies ... long stretches of difficult nailing sometimes on cheesy body-weight pancakes. Warren doesn't remember, but he actually took a pretty good fall when he ripped a string of RURPs. There were also long sections of drilled holes. Harding had us erase a lot of the route as we went up to reuse hangers, but a lot because he was so pissed off about that whole *Wall of Early Morning Light* thing. Chopping his own route was sort of his way of raising his finger at [Royal] Robbins."

Bosque's last remark refers to *the* Yosemite controversy. In 1970, Harding completed a 27-day first ascent of the *Wall of Early Morning Light* on El Capitan. His ascent polarized the climbing community over a perceived excess of bolting and media attention. Two months later, Royal Robbins and Don Lauria deliberately took a cold chisel to the first four pitches. Higher up, Robbins refrained from further erasure in part because the climbing was actually difficult, and because the damage was done. Harding "could never figure out what was wrong with the route," and took the chopping to heart by stripping the rivets and bolts off the Porcelain Wall.

Eric has projected a course tackling the imposing sweep to the right of *The Harding/Bosque/Lomba.* The passage would link features up a 900-foot slab and then through a cresting 1000-foot headwall. His line is a shimmering progression of cracks, corners, and seams separated by several lengthy blank sections. When I arrive in the Valley, Eric has already fixed four slab pitches and hauled hardware to the high point.

My first lead kicks off with hard, low-angle face moves on crumbly edges. One hundred feet of free and aid take me to a wet tension traverse. At the end of the traverse a pair of pine trees grow straight up and out of the horizontal gash that divides the slab from the headwall. Dark ooze leaks out from around the trunks and stains the lower face in fecal streaks. The trees are the obvious end to the pitch, and also a perfect lasso target. The big pins clipped to the end of my trail line ping off the face and rattle back down, but persistence pays off and a few clanks later I'm jugging the left pine. It sways to and fro.

The pine's trunk is several feet around at its base and sopping wet. I daisy in. I bounce in aiders and watch the needled branches sway to the rhythm. *SHOOMP* — everything slips a few inches. The tree is pulling out. I quickly tie off the right-hand pine, but paranoia tells me it's no good either.

Eric jugs up to me then casts off with a series of shaky stems

67

between the right tree and the wall. The pine creaks like an arthritic joint.

"This anchor sucks," I warn. "Don't push too hard or we're history."

Eric shoots me a placating look. "Yeah, huh. Maybe I could just put a bolt in, like the famous *Drill Sergeant,*" he says, referring to a long-time Yosemite climber who Kohl considers possessed with adding bolts to established routes.

From his stem 20 feet up, Eric eases onto marginal gear and then hooks to the next obstacle, a colossal inverted staircase similar to the "huge plates ... one pasted to the next and each hollow as can be," that Harding had encountered. Each blow of Eric's hammer is followed by a hollow *whump.* Conservative A3+, he says.

As I clean the pitch, the fleeting orange light of evening imparts a vitality to lifeless things. A shout echoes from the west. It's Greg Epperson taking photos. Epi, who has worked with me on several big-wall photo projects, can't seem to get enough punishment. Today he dangles by a thread on a broken buttress to the east. His thin shout reaches us, "Why don't you guys *do* something?"

Epi wants some action. No thanks, we've already gotten ours. The headwall above is as continuously steep as the belly of a supertanker, and there's about 1000 feet of it. For us, it's bivy and a beer.

Night falls. Somewhere out left is Harding's route, with its hard nailing and chopped ladders. At the base we had found evidence of the deconstruction: small zinc rivets and mashed plumber's-tape hangers.

Despite or perhaps because of the controversy surrounding him, Harding is still held in high esteem by the iconoclastic characters of Yosemite. Mulish independence and a penchant for wine have endeared him to many Valley climbers. When I spoke to him about the Porcelain Wall he said, "It was a hell of a lot of work ... scary as anything I'd been on. Continuously overhanging with ledges strewn with big loose blocks. I remember one time I got one foot up on a ledge, reached up and grabbed a four-foot by four-foot block. [Chuckles] It almost came off and me with it, so I put a few bolts in and tied it to the wall with some webbing. I wonder if that webbing is still holding it there."

68

Lying in my portaledge that night I think about the seven years I spent in Yosemite and how the wild rollercoaster life of big-wall climbing led to my wife Charisse. I fall asleep and dream about Charisse, Iowa, and vast, flat expanses of green.

Next morning my shift starts with flexy pin placements to heads and a hook. The hook is seated on a crisp flake that jogs up and right and merges with a larger plate puzzle-pieced into the wall proper. I rap the wall. TOOM. TOOM. "Even if I wanted to drill, the rivet wouldn't be worth squat," I mutter, not that Eric would care even if he heard me. He is deep in his Walkman. Even so, a few stray words sneak past the yellow noise filter. He thinks I'm mouthing off, looking for a reason to bail.

"You are finishing your pitch," he says and replaces the head-phones.

"Yeah. No shit," I reply.

We have entered a pale, white circle of granite, a fresh scar from a 1987 rockfall when a titanic 350-foot obelisk peeled away from the wall. The dotted line of Kohl's route climbs straight into the destruction.

Creaky hooks and thin nailing lead to a multi-tiered roof festooned with large stone danglers — the Death Cookies. Des Moines starts to sound pretty good. I clear a path by hucking Frisbee-sized flakes. The missiles shriek a good 20 feet out from Eric's head. I pick my way like a cat in cactus. My right foot scrapes the broken skin of the old Porcelain Wall; my left boot skates against the new Porcelain Wall laid bare after entombed eons.

The chunks become too heavy for me to toss. I can only influence their general flight path with a nudge. Eric snaps to attention — for the first time he is actually watching me. Two fist jams and I am topstepping, shoving a number three Camalot behind a flake. I forcefully bounce test the Camalot and watch in horror as sand and pebbles skitter out from behind the flake. The entire 40-foot-high feature is expanding.

"What's going on?" Eric yells.

"This is really weird!"

"Looks like A1 to me."

"Shuttup. This whole friggin' thing is moving!"

Eric says nothing. In 1990 he and Walt Shipley did the first ascent of El Cap's *Surgeon General,* a sporty A5 just right of *Zodiac.* High on the *Surgeon* Shipley led an expanding pitch that creaked and groaned under his weight. An alarmed Walt voiced his concern. Kohl's response? "Straighten out your bloomers and shut up." They completed the route without mishap but several years later the whole pitch parted company with the face, obliterating fixed gear on several routes.

An hour later I drill a belay, and I'm happy that Eric now gets to lead us out of the Circle of Death. I am not happy about the 200-pound dingleberries that dangle directly overhead.

"This is worse than *Bushido,*" Eric says.

Great. *Bushido* is a notorious Jim Bridwell outing on Half Dome that he once described as so loose it was, "A route I would not will upon my worst enemy."

Eric weaves left through shattered rock and reaches a shallow overhanging dihedral perpendicular to the roof. He is up and right of the belay.

"You're a Christian, right?" he asks.

"Yeah," I reply, half expecting a jest.

"That means if we are up here together we won't die, right?"

"When it's time to go, it's time to go. Just be ready."

"Yeah. Right," says Eric, then shrugs and beats a RURP to the hilt. The dingleberries vibrate.

"Be careful ... you're looking good," I shout.

Eric navigates a complex series of overlaps without a word or a bolt. He drills a belay as dusk casts its merciful tint on the face. Before sleep takes me I trace the outline of a huge fin, loose, of course, that hangs directly overhead like the Sword of Damocles.

Eric is one of those guys who is little known outside Yosemite. For those in the know he is considered one of the most accomplished hard aid climbers ever. He is abrasive and smart. He knows how to push peoples' buttons and will do so unrelentingly if the mood strikes him. Once he told me I was a "stupid nigger who didn't know how to set up a portaledge" when I mentioned that a portaledge he had sold me kept collapsing and I eventually had to throw it away. On the Porcelain Wall, however, I see a mellower, more gentle Eric. Has some woman recently dragged him through the dirt? Or has his outlook on climbing changed, after all, Eric hasn't lived in the Valley for a few years and after this summer he's going to study radiology in the Bay Area. He wants to specialize in fluoroscopic music video production. Perhaps at Eric's level of play you either quit and do something else, or you don't quit and die.

Myself, I either move to Iowa or ruin my marriage.

The next day Harding's words, incessant as the tapping of my hammer, ring in my mind. "We did some long ladders. We broke a lot of bits. The stone was quite formidable." Another bit snaps in the middle of my long rivet ladder. This section averages 93 degrees, a cresting wave of gray ceramic. Strenuous drilling. The stone is case-hardened with a dark, baked glaze. Eric and I are aiming for a huge, blond, upright, oval we have dubbed the Yellow Planaria. Out right sits Epi, a bored-looking dot in the corner of my eye. Pitch 10 ends after eight hours. Thirty rivets. 195 feet.

On day four Eric climbs a short rivet ladder to natural hooking out a bulge. After a brief head groove, and several enhanced (Kohl prefers to call them "enchanted") hooks, he is swimming with the Yellow Planaria. The corner is a seam that barely accepts Beak tips. Occasionally the crease blinks to Lost Arrow size. Eric uses every blade, Bugaboo and Beak on the rack. Modern A4. I am jealous cleaning the beautiful and difficult pitch. It is one of the best stretches of aid ever.

My next pitch is one of the worst. Scary trundling, a short bit of A3 hooking and nailing, and then a *very* long ladder.

At our bivy atop the Planaria we discuss how such a feature came to exist.

"Why is this thing all yellow?" I ask.

"It's dusted with uranium ore," Kohl responds.

"You mean it's radioactive?"

"Yeah, and you're going sterile right now."

I change the subject. "What makes you want to quit all this and go to school?"

"I don't know. I just need something to do besides climb. I'm getting cooked on all this wall-climbing slavery. I want to sit on the beach, get a tan, and look at girls."

"Yeah, and this will always be here," I say, gesturing down valley.

"Yeah, sure," Eric mutters, "You can always come back."

During his Yosemite career, Eric has completed 24 Grade VI first ascents, about half solo and all but three A4 or A5. Only two or three of his routes have seen second ascents: Kohl routes are typically loose and expanding. Some of these creations he is quite proud of. There's *Reckless Abandon* (VI 5.8 A4+) and *World of Pain* (VI 5.8 A5), both on the Yosemite Falls Wall and typical Kohl: twisted, dangerous, minimal drilled holes. Some of his less-proud renditions like *Hole World* (VI 5.10 A4) link not-so-classic climbing with long ladders. At the height of his first-ascent phase Kohl had told me that, "I'm not in the business of putting up public-service routes. I don't see the point."

I finish my loathsome pitch the next day. Our target now is a huge ledge, hopefully our last bivy. We are pretty psyched and figure Epi, who has been hanging on ropes shooting for the past week, has had about enough of the Porcelain Wall as well.

The end is in sight. Tonight we occupy a large, rubble-strewn ledge tastefully decorated with dresser-size blocks. Far to the left, a surprise, I can see the tattered remnants of a chopped Harding ladder. In the middle of a large flake an old quarter-inch bolt pokes through a corroded hanger. Here, Harding, Bosque, and Lomba bivied nearly 20 years earlier. We are the second party to sleep on the shelf where Harding "put in a bunch of bongs and things in a crack to anchor ourselves. That damn wall was so weird that the next morning every pin had fallen out. It was a good thing we were on a ledge." Eric and I drill a good rivet on the right side to back up the anchors.

We pass the night in relative comfort, swapping stories and telling jokes like we're inmates, about to receive an early release. The topics soon get serious.

"It's almost easier up here," I say. "That down there is a whole world of hurt."

It is dark. We watch the flickering lights of traffic and campers at Curry Village and the Yosemite Lodge. The tourists and locals are busy, doing their lives.

"Nobody's innocent," says Eric.

"Yeah. How does knowing that make you feel?"

"I don't know. Seems like everybody kinda gets what they deserve," replies Eric.

"If that is true, then what do you deserve?"

"I don't know," Eric says, then laughs. "I guess I deserve to be up here with the likes of you."

Thinking of life in Des Moines, I carry on, "I believe that God gives us what we need, not what we want. The rest is up to us."

"How are we supposed to know what we need?" Eric says, laughing. It is a rhetorical question. His face is barely discernible in the dark.

"I guess it's sorta like the Lotto," I reply. "You can't win if you don't play."

The next day begins with a lasso session. Eric tries to toss a hook over a large flake, 20 feet above.

"We need one of those grappling hooks," he says.

Fresh out of grappling hooks, he drills. Several holes later he hand traverses the flake and proceeds up a 93-degree wall, linking loose scythe-like flakes with rivets and hooks. He belays just short of the summit. I wince, cleaning the pitons from behind banana-shaped flakes that resonate with dull complaint as the pins slide out.

Eric watches as I approach the final pin placements driven diagonally under a completely detached six-by-five-foot scab. The flake is cemented in place with sand. I jerk a blade back and forth, my other hand on the scab to keep it in place.

"You were crazy to stand on that."

"Epi told me it was OK," says Eric. "I think he wanted to take pictures of someone getting killed."

Epi shrugs, "Not my job to interfere."

I lead the last pitch, enchanting hooks with drill and hammer. The end is classic — a funky mantel on an incut summit. On top we shake hands. We're both glad it's over. Another wall with Eric? Sure. I gaze east and think of corn.

First published in Climbing *No. 162, September 1996.*

The Mad Cow
The Stevie Haston situation

Y ou are nothing but a slant-eyed bastard," the man says. I recline in my chair, patiently fold my hands, and attempt an air of Oriental inscrutability. If I am to be insulted, I might as well play the part. Across the table sits Stevie Haston, a man I've just met. We are at the local pub in Ouray, Colorado. It's the final evening of the 1997 Ouray Ice Festival.

Haston leans forward, closing in. The black eyes stalk me. Crablike, he encircles a dark pint glass with hands and arms.

"What I am saying," he continues, "is that where I come from, you would be called a slant-eyed bastard every day. Where I grew up everyone called us criminals. If you get called something enough, that's what you become. Know what I mean?"

I know. I meet Haston's stare. There's no malice there. Just a statement of fact.

An hour earlier, Haston had completed a rousing slide presentation fueled by beer after beer and accompanied by sharp, profane narrative. Black humor laced the whole production. He gave a searing critique of climbing's status quo, with remarks generating as much nervous chuckling as true laughter in the crowded hall.

The projector cast dark images of a shape fighting through gray overhangs laced with menacing crystal shards. Then, swelling the screen and cresting like tidal waves, came deep blue seracs. "These fickle monsters," Stevie boldly declared, "are the future of pure ice climbing." A dozen slides later came a sequence of Haston gaffing a hollow pillar, Grade 6+. First, he was a red dot gingerly pecking at the thin veneer, dwarfed by the huge ice column, tools punching through brittle eggshell with every hit. When he was 90 feet up the second pitch, the tube collapsed. Haston rode it down past his belayer all the way to the base of the first pitch. His partner was certain that Haston had died, crushed under many tons of ice. Then, on the screen and very much alive, was a dark figure straddling a shattered log of ice. It was Stevie Haston, grinning.

Haston's closed the show with a shot at the media. "If there are any climbing-magazine editors in the audience, I challenge you to bloody well watch who your heroes are."

Stevie Haston, 40, has been butting heads with the established order most of his life. In the climbing world he is often perceived as antagonistic and divisive. His first lecture was delivered at the 1996 DMM British Mountain Festival. Of the 1500 attendees, at least 100 walked out, offended. One who stayed was Ian Smith of the British magazine *High,* who wrote that Haston had, "a gentle meditative delivery, almost spiritual, but [with] the content deeply acerbic and critical ... Stevie is planning to extend his lecturing, if he does and you get the chance to see him, grab it."

Many climbers dismiss Stevie Haston as just an obnoxious Brit, but their basis has more to do with his character than track record. Those who know him well defend Haston with a loyalty reserved for family members. Kyle Lefkoff, a Boulder investor who first met Haston in the 1970s in Wales, says: "Stevie will always elicit reactions. That's how he was when I first met him and that's how he is now. It seems like people either love him or hate him. One thing is certain, everyone has an opinion."

Haston's has been a long and phenomenal climbing career, though the quality and volume of his accomplishments have not found corresponding recognition with the general public, or the sponsors who make large-scale climbing dreams a reality. In a recent profile for the British climbing magazine *On the Edge,*

Martin Crook asked, "Why aren't the magazines full of him? Why have you barely heard of him? How come he's not been on every major Himalayan trip in the last 15 years?" Perhaps because the fervor that has sustained three decades of top-notch performance also burned his social bridges.

At the tender age of 16, Haston soloed the *Col du Plan Direct* (M4) above Chamoix, in winter. In his late teens, he was Britain's leading alpinist. His solo list now totals more than 60 climbs up to ED+ (hard, mixed, and exposed) in the Alps. When he was 20, Haston, partnered with Victor Saunders, and climbed the Eiger's North Face in winter. On rock, in the 1970s and early 1980s Haston soloed up to 5.12a and did numerous ground-up firsts, some rated 5.12+, often runout. In 1980 he put up the first Grade 7 ice route in the world: the *Terminator* in North Wales. His current resume lists multitudes of hard redpoints including *Maginot Line* (5.14b), 5.13b on-sights — like *Pourquoi pas* in Volx, and *Shaoshing* and *Hegel* in Ceuse — 7000-meter peaks, 5.13b at 4400 meters, and 5.14a high in the Alps. Last winter, Haston's notoriety exploded in the United States when he established mixed climbs as hard as any here, made rapid repeats of other mixed testpieces, and freed extreme desert climbs. Says Will Gadd, a leading mixed climber, "He's like a chunk of climbing history still in action."

Says Haston, "I'm not a hero. I'm just a climber who tries harder than most."

From childhood, Haston learned to try hard — at first just to survive. "I grew up in a criminal part of London, the East End. I also had some trouble because me mum was rather dark. Me father, on the other hand, was quite white — you know, like a fucking albino. As you can see, I'm a bit in the middle."

Haston is fair-skinned, with piercing black eyes that dart back and forth when he's animated. When he is provoked, they ignite with dark rage. When he's happy a wide grin splits his face and the eyes melt into pools of mirth. At 5' 8", his variable weight fits into a broad-shouldered yet compact frame. He has a buccaneer's hawkish profile and long jet-black hair tied back in an oily knot.

Haston's father was a tough Scot. In an *On The Edge* profile he remembered: "I tried to gain love and respect in my father's eyes but he'd done it all already: grown up in Edinburgh — the poor part — in the '30s, been a cook's boy on whaling ships, led a mutiny in W.W.II on his merchant ship and strikes in the construction industry in London. He used to tell me of knife fights in Zanzibar brothels and lions walking down the street. It's really sad now that he's old and paralyzed, all that strength gone."

From his mother's roots Haston received a gift that would last a lifetime: climbing. Reprieve from the stifling East End came during summer holidays with her relatives in Malta. Stevie says: "I first climbed there with me granddad. We would go fishing and scramble about on these cliffs. That's where I first felt a love for climbing." Haston laughs when he thinks of his grandfather. "He was a great man. I remember begging him to teach me to swim, so the bastard grabs me and throws me into the sea. It was sink or swim."

Violence, alcohol, and crime were an integral part of the scenes of Haston's youth. A paternally ingrained toughness and stubborn self-reliance dropped Stevie into trouble on a regular basis. He won his way into an exclusive grammar school, only to be expelled after tossing the headmaster across a room. Haston is not proud of those events. He only says, "If you treat a human like a kid, you will create a kid. If you treat a human like a criminal, you create a criminal."

At 21, he broke a man's leg in five places. "His brothers threatened to kill me," he recalls. "I took it a bit seriously because one of them was in prison for stabbing somebody." To defend himself, he took up Kung Fu and entered pseudo-legal full-contact fights until his martial-arts instructor, Allan Whittal, got knifed to death in the street.

Haston battled even harder to flourish as a climber. From his first days of cutting class and hitchhiking to the crags, he was never content with an average performance. He attacked climbing as he would attack an opponent in a brawl. Jim Perrin, a leading British climber of the 1970s, recalls: "I remember this little kid comes breezin' up to Wales, obnoxious, hugely confident, and absolutely wonderful. Stevie was a joy to those who could see his talent. On the rock he was always head down and straight-on-in."

The late 1970s and early 1980s were a heyday for British rock climbing, both in technical standards and boldness. As one of the original climbers on the dole, Haston had plenty of time to indulge his passion to climb, and soon developed a reputation for ox-like strength and pit-bull tenacity. A veteran British climber, Dave Towse, recalls an early ascent of Ron Fawcett's runout *Hall of Warriors*, on Dinas Cromlech at Llanberis Pass. The route clocked in at E5 6a (5.11d/12a), a ferocious grade at the time. Towse remembers: "There goes Stevie up this steep rock with some sketchy gear. He lunges up, gets a hold, but can't move up. He yells down, 'Watch me, Dave!' Then he comes off. I'm nestled down, cringing at the belay, waiting for him to land on top of me. I look up and there's Stevie hanging on some holds below the high point. Seems he jumped off and grabbed the rock as he fell. As you can tell, even back then he was quite strong."

Haston found the emerging sport climbs of the mid-1980s to be not only an end in themselves but, more so, a means — to train for ground-up desperates. Several of his bold first ascents have only recently been repeated. *Isis is Angry* (E7 6c, 5.12d R/X) lies on the steep loose South Stack of the Welsh sea cliff Gogarth. The guidebook description for *Isis* states, "Looking for trouble? This route takes no prisoners." Mike "Twid" Turner, a recent Gogarth activist, describes the first pitch as requiring "prayer and botanical stress analysis to teeter up its conglomerate rubble ... probably the South Stack's most serious pitch." *My Secret Garden* (E6 6b, 5.12c R/X) resides on an even steeper, looser land, the Llyen Peninsula in Wales. It's only recently seen a repeat after more than 10 years.

Some of Stevie's first ascents became mega-classics, like *Comes the Dervish* (E3 6a, 5.11a) in North Wales. Others never achieved classic status because they didn't last long enough. Two Haston firsts literally fell down. *Fear of Rejection* (E6 6a) was a completely unprotected 5.11+ offwidth. *Lost Castle* had good gear, but its grade of E7 (5.13a) added spice. Haston is particularly sad about *Lost Castle's* demise because it was a route of unique disposition (four-inch to nine-inch, flared, and overhanging 30 feet in 80). It toppled over before getting a second ascent. He says: "I could never figure out why no one wanted to do it."

To him, the character, ambiance, and location of routes supersede pure difficulty. In 1994 he redpointed *Maginot Line* (8c, 5.14b) and on-sighted a slew of 7c+ and 8a's. When I press him on the significance of these ascents, Haston dismisses them with a wave, saying, "I'll tell you, mate, bolt climbing is all about losing weight and working out. A hard bolt route is nice but not nearly as memorable as a hard ice or alpine climb. I was so miserable when I was working on *Maginot Line*. It came down to whether I could hold an 1/8-inch hold for about a second. It took me five mornings, which was better than Ben Moon and pretty good for someone who is not a Chris Sharma. Think about it, mate, *Amphibian* is more interesting than *Maginot Line* by a hundred miles."

Amphibian is Will Gadd's 1997 mixed rock and ice testpiece, consisting of Rifle-steep limestone punctuated with the occasional ice goatee. It takes an outrageous line straight out the steepest section of the Fang amphitheater at Vail. When *Amphibian* was originally reported at the stratospheric grade of M10, Haston, then residing in Chamonix, took notice. He recalls, "I had just completed two routes in Italy which I thought quite hard, *009* and *Welcome to the Machine*. I thought both to be M9. Being the keen sportsman that I am, I woke up in the middle of the night and said to meself, 'I'm getting a ticket to the States to climb *Amphibian*.'"

In a two-day effort, Haston repeated *Amphibian*, the first redpoint of which had taken weeks of preparation. He bumped the grade down to solid M9 and in doing so, confirmed his efforts in Italy as equal to the world standard in mixed climbing.

By coming to the States and snagging the second ascent, Haston demonstrated two things. First, he put himself in the forefront of the mixed game by having established or repeated the hardest mixed climbs at the crags and in the mountains (his 1995 route, *Scotch on the Rocks* on Mont Blanc du Tacul in the French Alps, was confirmed in 1996 as M8 when François Damailano and partner were forced to resort to aid on the crux section). Second, the ascent reflects his desire to be challenged on an international level.

"If you don't travel, you stagnate," he says. "How can you grow if you are afraid to get out? The same can be said of a man if he is a racist or if he is parochial in his outlook. Such men are doomed. The same goes for climbing."

Haston's mixed achievements are a specialized extension of an alpine career that started when he was 15. Every year, Haston would scrounge money for an annual trip to Chamonix. His record of climbs is a laundry list of solos and firsts. Mark Twight, a leading American alpinist and former Chamonix resident, recalls: "I know he's soloed at least 40 routes TD or harder. He is one of the best all-around climbers I've ever seen. All these great stories surround him. One time in '85, I think, he hitched down from England in shorts and a T-shirt. Then he borrowed some gear, put GoreTex over his shorts, and went and soloed a big route. On it, he got caught in a storm, rescued two German climbers — and went on to the top."

By the early 1990s, Haston was surrounded by a growing catalog of wild tales extraneous to climbing. Like the time he broke a man's leg who threatened him at a hotel pub, or his battles with the French Gendarmes at Snell's Field in Chamonix. Stevie is not randomly aggressive. His skirmishes always come with plenty of provocation from the opposite party. He is just less tolerant of abuse than most.

Never one to ingratiate himself with the chauvinistic and nationalistic French alpine scene, Stevie has lately gained the nickname *La Vauche Folle,* or mad cow. The name refers to the mad-cow disease that plagued the British meat industry and became, for the French, an unwanted English import. It is ironic, then, that the most influential person in Haston's life is French. In 1990, Haston moved to Chamonix to live with his wife-to-be, Laurence Gouault. She runs the Patagonia shop in Chamonix and is herself a tremendous climber. Gouault leads Grade 6 ice, flashes 5.12, and recently made light work of the hardest mixed route in France, Jean Christophe Lafaille's *Les Compres* (M7+) near Chamonix. Haston describes Gouault simply as, "My woman and my best partner."

Says Kyle Lefkoff, "Over the years, I've seen a lot of Stevie's relationships come and go. Out of all Stevie's wives, Laurence is the best of the bunch. She is a great stabilizing influence. I think it's great that Stevie comes to France, snags the hardest rock and ice climbs in the Chamonix area, and then steals this French beauty."

Haston's dealings with the opposite sex have had their share of strife. By the time he was 26 he'd had two wives and fathered three children. Haston illustrates the end of one affair with a typical tall tale:"It's like this. I was in love with this woman, see. One day she says to me, 'I can't love you because you are crazy.' So I ask her, 'What do you mean I'm crazy?' She says, 'I think you are schizophrenic.' So I grab her by the neck, and say, 'Exactly, I am crazy. I've got all these personalities. Why can't you love at least one of them!'"

Haston loves his children and has an extra-close relationship with his oldest daughter, Katie. Stevie, Laurence, and Katie often climb together in France and Wales. Katie, 16, climbs 5.11+ trad routes and on-sights 7b at the sport crag. In a recent mini-interview in yet another British magazine, *Climber,* she showed her own bit of Haston cockiness, poking fun at her father. When asked about developing a climbing form she replied, "Well, I ignore my dad's advice about doing weights and pull-ups, so my physique is just from climbing outside and sessions at the wall."

Says Lefkoff, who has seen Katie develop over the years: "Her mother is Welsh, so she has this ingrained resourcefulness. When they climb together Stevie is always worried that she'll burn him off. Who knows? Maybe one day she will. Just like her dad, Katie will be a great climber and heart breaker."

Living in Chamonix provided Haston the opportunity to do first ascents of extreme cascades like Nuit Blanches and Cascade Les Geurs, both Grade 7. Close proximity to big mountains facilitated free solos of hard alpine routes — including a winter ascent of the Walker Spur in eight hours. Haston also established several very difficult rock climbs, including the hardest route in the area, the 8b+ Sans Liberté in 1996.

In France, Haston continued a legendary training regimen he began in England. He says a typical day might include up to 2000 pull-ups, 3000 pushups, and one-arm pull-ups with a 35-pound dumbbell in the other hand. These incredible numbers along with the volume and difficulty of his climbing have led some climbers to doubt his claims. Some of Stevie's recent desert free climbs, which have included *Phantom Spirit* (5.12 R) in the Fisher Towers, have been questioned by American climbers who are unwilling to be quoted. These questions are in part due to an uncharacteristic overgrading of some pitches by Haston, and the fact that some routes were witnessed only by Laurence. His other belayers vouch for him.

One story may illuminate, in part, the basis for doubts. Dave Towse recalls: "I was in Hueco Tanks with Stevie. We'd go bouldering and Stevie would be nowhere near doing this problem he was working on. He'd fall off and I thought, 'Oh, give it up. There's no way you're going to do it.' Then I'd turn around and he'd do it! He's a bit of an overachiever in that way. He definitely does not follow the same step-by-step process that we expect. I can see why some might doubt his ability."

Haston is no stranger to accusations of unethical behavior. He brings up an example. "Due to the longevity of my climbing, my body can change from one physique to another in three months' time. I weighed 135 pounds when I did *Maginot Line*. When I'm skiing or doing martial arts, I weigh 165 pounds. I can go from a good Himalayan climber to a good sport climber so fast that people in England think I'm on steroids. I think that's pretty funny! It's like this. I make damn sure I exploit all my talents. I'm not going to be 60 and wonder, 'What if?'"

Kyle Lefkoff says emphatically: "Stevie is a man of great integrity. When he says, 'I did such-and-such route on such-and-such day,' it is true. In social scenes and on certain non-serious subjects, Stevie can be a bullshitter. But not about serious climbing."

After his diatribe in Ouray, I don't see Stevie until he returns to the States to compete in the Winter X-Games in California. He stops along the way in Colorado, and we meet at the Hungry Toad in Boulder. The bar has the congenial atmosphere of a nice English pub and, as Stevie put it, "decent beer."

Sitting down, he embarks on a stream-of-consciousness monologue. First comes an update on his latest exploits in France. No surprise that the first yarn has nothing to do with climbing.

"I just got here from Chamonix," Haston says. "Laurence and I were in the telepherique and two men started making comments about her. Not knowing I speak French, they were a bit liberal in their comments."

"So then what happened?"

"Of course I had to beat 'em, mate."

Haston dives into the ale. Our discussion heats up as he rankles about the Association of British Mountain Guides, which recently denied him guide certification. When the narrative reaches its apex, Haston's voice rises several octaves. "Those bastards failed me because they didn't like me. Well, you know what, I don't give a fuck whether they like me or not!" The ale has been buffered only by a handful of nuts from the bar. I fidget as sedate patrons cast wary glances our way, and remember that Stevie was, at one point, banned from every pub in Llanberis for bad behavior — an amazing feat in a town where drinking is part of the traditional culture.

"It's like this," Stevie says darkly. He leans forward, casting a discreet eye left to right like a kid sharing a dirty joke. "I think of my future. I know I can't climb forever. I tried out for guide certification as a long-term way to make money. I am light leagues ahead of those twats, but they still failed me because of my attitude. Fancy that, my attitude, mate!"

Part of me finds it easy to see. By necessity, bureaucratic systems demand conformity, consistency, and compliance. Haston, rasping under the control of those with lesser climbing credentials, no doubt alienated some. Regarding Stevie's ability as a guide, Martin Crook wrote, "[Joe Brown and I] both agreed that when it came down to Joe's grandchildren, or my son William, the only person we'd consider using as a guide for them would be Stevie. Strikes me [the Association of British Mountain Guides] cracked under the pressure of coming face to face with authentic talent."

Raising yet another pint of Guinness, Haston changes subjects. His current home, Chamonix, finds no exemption from his biting criticism. It's no surprise that Haston has few French climbing partners. "In France they deify their climbers. They absolutely hate me because I can piss all over their hardest ice routes. In France they are so spoiled that if it's 10 minutes from the fucking road, they won't even climb it. J.C. Lafaille gets miles of press for his new mixed route, *Les Comperes*. I do it next, then I solo it, and then my wife leads it. [The French magazine] *Vertical* won't even publish a picture of me doing it!" Haston's voice drops to a conspiratorial level. "I tell ya, man, they don't have a clue about mixed climbing. Lafaille's route is only a bloody 7. Mixed climbing has two real homes, Colorado and Scotland, and the routes in Colorado are way ahead of Scotland.

"The Americans lead the mixed game, with the exception of myself, of course. The reason is simply because you have Jeff Lowe. You are free from nationalism and deeply ingrained bigotry. This results in an innovative and egalitarian scene. We can sit with someone like Jeff and we can all be chums. In Europe, someone like Jeff wouldn't even talk to us."

Haston has a soft spot in his heart for Lowe. He considers him a remarkable climber and kindred spirit who shares his passion for — and longevity in — climbing. Not that Lowe is, of course, safe from prodding. Haston jokes: "People say Jeff Lowe is the father of modern ice and mixed climbing. I would say he's more like the grandfather of modern ice and mixed. Know what I mean?"

Stevie is not so in love with American Himalayan climbing.

"I see Americans taking their expeditions in two directions. One is to climb big walls, fixing rope, aid climbing, and all that. I find it pathetic. The idea of bashing my way up something like Trango Tower is insane. And the whole idea of aid climbing is total retro nonsense. The other direction involves climbing 8000-meter peaks via easy routes with disclaimers like, first woman to climb this, or first American to climb all 8000-meter peaks in 10 years and that type of rubbish. I find that direction infinitely more pathetic."

When I attempt to defend hard aid as something he has never experienced, Stevie lurches back and forth like he's leaning into a headwind. The veins in his head bulge. Putting his pint down with deliberation and with a mixture of venom and contempt reserved for imbeciles, he asks, "Do you really think I couldn't climb A5 if I wanted to?"

Haston feels slighted and misunderstood by the powers that be, deliberately passed over for a fair piece of the sponsorship pie.

Last year, he wanted money to attempt an extreme new route, alpine style, on Nuptse. Haston felt that his superb technical ability and recent rapid ascents of 6500 and 7000 meter peaks (he did Shivling in nine hours) in the Garwhal Himalaya proved his merit. Perhaps a lack of renown in certain circles cost him. He rages that money went to better-known, better-funded climbers. "It's bloody nepotism, man! Sometimes I get so much built up inside, I just want to fucking explode!

"Any money that goes for the Himalayas goes to idiots on easy 8000-meter peaks. Do you know what an easy 8000-meter peak is? Perhaps you've heard of fell walking, mate? Everything is moving away from the technical edge. People should be trying harder things at altitude. Most people who do 8000-meter peaks are fat old men and useless twats. You might as well put a plastic bag over your head and do press-ups!"

Perhaps Haston is as known for abrasiveness as athleticism. Kyle Lefkoff says: "Most climbers are characteristically modest about their achievements. There is nothing modest about Stevie. He's putting it out there all the time."

Says Will Gadd of Haston's dilemma, "Ninety percent of the climbing world doesn't know him or care about what he does. It's sad because here's a fellow who is super talented and super accomplished, who, if he had the [positive] attitude of Alex Lowe, would be clocking up the sponsorship dollars. The crux for Stevie is not in the climbing, it's in the smiling."

Haston's attitude at the 1997 Winter X-Games, however, was a sparkling light among those who viewed the fledgling ice-climbing games with disdain or disappointment. Gadd, a fellow participant, says: "Nobody supported the other climbers like Stevie. He stayed when he didn't have to and he cheered everybody else even after a disappointing performance. He didn't implode like some of the others."

Haston's longtime friend and ardent supporter Jim Perrin says, "I love him dearly. But he is an obnoxious little twat. He is very insightful, very honest, and doesn't suffer fools. Stevie accepts his limitations and he is ready to push right up against them. He expects others to push up against their own boundaries also. That is where he gets misunderstood."

Haston is well aware of his shortcomings. "I am very impatient and intolerant. I have to work on these shortcomings and I am very conscious of them."

His future plans include hard free climbing in the Himalaya, more top-standard mixed climbing, routes like the unclimbed South Face of Lhotse, and alpine dreams that boggle the mind.

Raising up one vision, Haston says, "I dream of doing all the 8000-meter peaks in a year. That's what I asked (the sponsors) money for."

When I naively ask if he got the money, Stevie shoots me a look of utter incredulity.

"Are you fucking joking, man?"

The Hungry Toad is shutting down. Other patrons have left, though we never notice their departure. The bartender casts reproachful glances our way as we finish our pints. We step outside to share a cigarette. Haston lights up, draws deeply and offers the cigarette to me. I take it, raise it to my lips, and choke down a drag. I hack and pass the butt back, muttering: "I hate these things. But sometimes I just can't help myself." Stevie smiles knowingly. He lifts the insidious nub and inhales, the cherry glow softly bathing his face. He turns to me and says, "The Maltese have a saying — 'A man is a smoker before he is born.' Funny how that is. We can't always help being what we are."

First published in Climbing *No. 176, May 1998.*

The Good Earth
Tottering towers that redefine the word classic

Grand Junction, Colorado, isn't the hub of American climbing, but within a couple hours' drive you can be pulling limestone in Rifle Mountain Park, jamming sandstone towers in the Canyonlands, or nailing big walls in the Black Canyon of the Gunnison. The fall of 1992 found me in Junction, where my greatest trouble was finding psyched locals. Commuting to Rifle, where partners are plentiful, seemed a productive alternative to stagnation.

The road from Grand Junction to Rifle winds through layers of sandstone, granite, and shale, all in varying stages of decay. Just northeast of Palisade, sits Mount Garfield, a squat truncated mesa of dirt. The summit plateau is composed of reasonably sound sandstone. On the melting clay slopes below the plateau stand a handful of ephemeral spires, crumbling summits 10 to 200 feet high, some so narrow you can practically bear hug them. Helmeted shafts of mud sprout like giant mushrooms from slopes and ridges. Long shark fins soar upward sporting tooth-like crenellations of jagged blocks. The towers are here today, perhaps gone tomorrow.

I love bouldering. Simple, powerful, and unfettered. On one trip to Rifle, my partner and I pulled off I-70 for close inspection of the

89

sterile landscape of Mount Garfield. We had found good bouldering nearby, and I assumed, through simple optimistic extrapolation, that this blessed quality would extend throughout the region.

The results of close scrutiny were disappointing. Bad landings, bad rock, and bad location plagued the area. Most of the good stones were lying at acute angles on steep inclines — a slip would send you cartwheeling hundreds of feet down sharp talus and into the oncoming traffic of I-70. Other boulders lay out of reach, perched high on steep clay towers, some over a rope-length up ...

The most climbable formation appeared to be a squat tower in a narrow valley eye level with the interstate. Speeding due east, you can catch a brief glimpse of the tower tucked in the hollow. The tower stands 100 feet high and is 40 feet from buttress to buttress, reminiscent of a castle turret. The Fortress, as we dubbed it, is heavily defended by blank, vertical soil on all sides, save for a bridge of dirt connecting the west shoulder to a mud slope. Detailed inspection indicated a line of weakness up a short section of clay. Above that, the remaining solid capstone would likely succumb to conventional rock climbing technique for the last 25 of so feet. Casual — or so it seemed.

Grand Junctionite Joel Arellano was the best candidate for this excursion. He had followed some aid pitches in the Fisher Towers, so was obviously willing to grovel. One spring afternoon we strolled out to Garfield with dirty business in mind. The weather was overcast; a somber pall of gray clouds blended nicely with Garfield's earthy coat.

The first pin was a 1/2-inch angle in what would have been, in granite, a Lost Arrow crack. The fat pin sank to the eye with a tap of the hammer and wiggled out with a few shakes. I repeated the process using consecutively larger pins, until I'd wailed a 2-inch bong into the slot. The bong emitted a dull ring before rattling loose with a hollow clunk. I tried again. This time it sagged under body-weight but held. Bounce testing sent off dust sprays, but the piton seemed fairly secure in a placement that felt more like plastic ice than rock. Above lay 30 feet of 80-degree dirt with the occasional fist-sized sandstone tooth poking through the crusty mantle. A free attempt made zero headway. There weren't any cracks. What a pity, I thought, I'm going to have to drill.

Compared to granite, hand drilling in sandstone is a leisure process. And this rock made drilling in sandstone feel like an athletic event.

I drilled a short ladder in 20 minutes, lowered off, and Joel took over. Fearlessly, he high stepped and plugged away like a pro. It was his first aid lead. After doling out basic instructions, I decided to have fun.

"Are ya scared, man?" I yelled.

"What?"

"I said ... ARE YOU SCARED!"

"Oh, I don't know."

"Whaddayamean, ya don't know?"

With the patient eyes and the patronizing tone of the annoyed, Joel replied, "Oh, I'm not really sure what there is to be scared of."

I'd forgotten that a minor hearing impairment was the only thing the prevented Joel from becoming a Navy SEAL.

I tried a different tack.

"How strong to you think those little pitons are in that dirt?"

"WHAT?" asked Joel now wide eyed.

"Oh, never mind," I smiled.

For the next 20 minutes I sat in smug silence. When Joel reached the capstone he lowered off and I resumed the lead. A light drizzle fell, keeping down the dust and leaving us pondering the effect of moisture on the already unstable medium. As I gazed up at the last 25 feet, a dull rumble rolled across us from an adjoining gully.

"What's up with that?"

Joel answered, "Oh, the top of one of these things just fell off."

Great. I nervously eyeballed the protection, a shallow drilled angle at foot level. The summit was a collection of thin sandstone plates, loosely stacked like shingles on a tile roof. I high stepped onto a crumbly plate resting on a sloping shelf. The plate disintegrated and I flicked the debris off with my toe.

"Gaaaaa!"

A hideous gray-green nightmare writhed near my toe, seeking shelter from the light. The centipede was at least four inches long — twisting, crawling — a trillion legs and inquisitive feelers waving in devilish unison.

"Huh?" Joel queried, cool but concerned.

The hammer came out. The centipede and his immediate surroundings were demolished in a miniature Hiroshima. The rubble trickled down. Joel looked up and caught some in the face.

"What's up?" he asked.

"Oh, nothin'," I innocently replied.

He shrugged, looked down, and flicked something green off his face. Ten minutes later I pitched a plate-sized wafer of sandstone over my shoulder trying to clear a decent mantle shelf onto the capstone.

It was the weirdest summit I had been on. It felt like it moved. The top was a loose mix of kitty-litter gravel interspersed with friable sandstone wafers that gave me the creeps. I drilled an anchor, fixed the rope, and Joel nipped up lickety split. Under Joel's hammer, the drilled angles released with a mere sigh. I could laugh, now that it was over. What a ridiculous route — a bodyweight bolt ladder with loose 5.9 free climbing. How do you grade that?

I was finding the towers attractive. Their transitory composition lends them a strange and formidable beauty. The summits are isolated and unique. Plus, there were no queues at the base.

Finding a psyched partner for new adventures was a bit of a task. No one I could find in Junction had the combination of willingness and competence to carry the torch. After the Fortress, Joel was only interested in more orthodox climbs. Then I discussed the area with Duane Raleigh.

Duane is no stranger to the desert. On his desert resume are numerous first ascents and hard repeats. Recently, Duane and his wife Lisa have established several speed records in the Fisher Towers. But achievement doesn't come without sobering reminders of what can happen. Seven years earlier, while descending from a new route on the Organ in Arches National Park, Duane fell out of a rappel. A 9-mm haul line, clipped to the gear rack, tangled and snagged in a crack, arresting him after a 150-foot free fall.

It was years before Duane returned to the desert, but when he did the I-70 towers were first on his agenda, and, as far as I know, he is one of the few climbers to actually get out of the car and scope the cliffs. He even had a classic line picked out on a wedge of mud dubbed the Mantis. All he was waiting for was a partner.

The Mantis is a thin rib of clay crested by a precarious series of isolated blocks. The blocks, perched on raised clay mounds, resemble bug eyes, lending an insect-like appearance. The 180-foot formation is split clean through by a crack. The fissure, ranging from knifeblade to four inches, was the objective and was a "near classic on a majestic pile," said Duane.

The short hike to the "worst climbing area in the world" took us through alien, blasted terrain. The desiccated ground was littered with broken glass, spent shell casings, and assorted animal bones. The twisted skyline lent an erriness to the air.

"I hate it here," Duane moaned. "I only climb here because I have to. I wish someone would put me out of my misery."

I, too, failed to see the glamour in clawing up these towers. They were ephemeral at best and their only redeeming qualities were their untouched summits and bizarre geometry.

We dumped our packs at the base. The rack was the usual selection of desert gear: angles, Leepers, bongs, cams, etc. Absent were nuts, heads, and hooks, all of which were worthless in the clay. In their place we carried a few innovative extras, such as aluminum tent stakes and Spectre ice pitons. I was glad that Duane was on the sharp end; someone had to see if those things would hold.

The damp of spring showers held the stinging dust to a minimum. But it also gave birth to raging hordes of black gnats that went straight for the ears, nose, and scalp. Duane's wife, Lisa, who had come along to partake in the festivities, was driven back to the shelter of the car. I was near bagging the business myself. Trouble was that I was stuck belaying Duane, who claimed that the bugs thinned out as he gained altitude. The constant piercing buzz and stinging bites forced me to tuck my arms and head under my shirt. Buttoned down, I belayed for nearly three hours as Duane pushed to the 100-foot mark using Spectres, which worked great, and bongs. The tent stakes bounced out.

At that point, all the three- and four-inch pins were used up, and we were even out of large Camalots, which when fully retracted, miraculously held despite shifting and flexing in the crumbling uneven crack. There was nothing left to do. Duane established a tenuous lower off, cleaned the lower gear, and we were gone.

Our little jaunt left us both taxed. Many days would pass before the horror subsided. The profusion of oozing gnat bites festered, scabbed, and then the itching recurred with renewed violence. This persistent irritation exacerbated the grim thoughts of the project looming overhead.

Half a year later, Duane and I returned to finish the Mantis. In the cool of late winter the area was free of gnats. One-hundred-seventy feet of steep aiding led to a summit with no capstone. To descend, Duane tied the haul line to the lead rope and rappelled off the opposite side of the tower using my body as a counter-weight. To clean, I jumared the lead rope using his body as an anchor, and, for fear of being slingshotted off the tower, didn't dare peek over the summit ridge.

On our next trip it was my turn on the sharp end. In previous weeks I had called shops on the West Coast and secured a large number of the magical Leeper-Zs and steel bongs. Armed with these out-of-production extras, I embarked on the 140-foot north face of the Fortress — the object of my initial foray. Choosing a gently overhanging line that started in a rough crack system leading to a blank section studded with jagged sandstone rocks, I hoped it would be solid enough to tie off. The crack went with the usual slow-burning white-knuckle tension on Spectres, Leeper stacks, and angles. At the end of the crack I looped a TV-sized block, half hoping it wouldn't hold long enough to test. The thought of riding out a ground fall tied to a 100-pound stone wasn't appealing. For several minutes I halfheartedly set and reset the slipping tie-off. The sling just would not stay in place. I resorted to the secret weapon.

Hilti makes a great drill. That, coupled with Duane's contribution to the war effort, a foot-long bit and 10-inch torque bolts, made for proud bolting. The first bolt tapped in nicely, and even appeared to tighten, as the clay on that section was reasonably compact. I clipped the aider and weighted the bolt. It oozed out a good quarter of an inch. I reversed onto the lower pin and screwed down the bolt even tighter. This time it stayed in place. Six holes later, the juice in the battery pack was worn down. Not bad — 60 inches of 1/2-inch hole on one battery.

A couple weeks passed before I sucked up the gumption to return. This time I didn't even bother with the cobbles. The shaky bolt ladder was more than enough. From an ethical point of view I wasn't concerned — who was going to complain about a handful of holes punched into a dirt wall?

Jeff Jackson, of Austin, Texas, belayed. He and his wife, Christina, were out sampling Rifle limestone. While bagging routes there, my lurid tales of unclimbed towers set the hook in his mouth. Like ourselves, he found the area repulsive, yet attractive. In fact, Jeff was the only climber who actually liked Mount Garfield. "It's no wonder he likes it. He's from Texas. They're used to bugs and dead things down there," said Duane, a native Oklahoman.

While I decompressed after topping out on the Fortress, Duane and Jeff ran over to a spire called the Turkey Neck. Duane has a tendency to fixate on the most outrageous — or grievous — lines in an area. The Turkey Neck was no exception. It rises out of a hillside like a giant raspy gizzard with a house-sized capstone overhanging on all sides. A shallow chimney flare split the upper shaft of the "neck." Duane's goal was to gain this feature using a rude mix of unorthodox aid and full-bore ice gear.

When I made it to the base Duane was in full armor. Plastic Koflach boots, monopoints, and recurve X-15s. In the 95-degree heat he took off, dry tooling and front pointing in shorts and tank top. After a scary series of lunges and loose-block pulls, he reached a band of vertical, unconsolidated dirt. The ice tools began to pull, pins failed, and even the lengthy bolts would barely hold. Spectres gained a few body lengths, putting him temptingly close to the flare. And terribly close to augering a deep hold at the base. I was getting sick just watching.

"Hey, man, I don't know, Duane."

"What?"

"It ain't looking good up there."

He retreated, to the disappointment and relief of us all, part downclimbing and part lowering off the shaky bolts.

Jeff was itching to take a crack at the short ridge and headwall ion the backside of the neck. We moved location to a sketchy platform opposite the connecting spine of mud. Jeff boldly stepped across and pulled a few aid moves. Here he was confronted with a crackless sheet of mud — the only barrier to the capstone. The recurve pick of a Lowe Bigbird slipped behind a detached flange of mud. A tenuous highstep on the tool gained the caprock and soon we were on top of the Turkey Neck. I was the last up, and once again was smitten with the oppressive vertigo I had felt on the Fortress.

We were all perched on a tiny rounded island balanced on a stalk of dried mud. The single bolt anchor added nothing to our sense of stability, and the island was abuzz with a legion of flying ants. Apparently, the ants had found sufficient solitude on this forsaken chunk of ground to get on with the serious business of reproduction. Our unexpected arrival sent them into a frenzy.

Uphill, the long shaft of the "Totem" was barely visible in the flickering light. To the left was the "Bug Eye," a sci-fi horror and irresistible challenge. Beyond that was the "Black Tower," a multipitch nightmare of jet-black clay. One valley over lurked the "Needle," with its three-foot-round shaft tapering to a two-foot-square capstone. All unclimbed.

Squinting through the fog of insect life, I locked onto Duane. He was leaning back, delivering himself to the void. He briefly glanced at the lone bolt, the rope, and our mere blob of a summit. I noticed he couldn't take his eyes off those pristine towers. With a sinking heart I knew we'd be back. That certainty hung over my head like an anvil — next time it was my lead.

First published in Climbing *No. 147, September 1994.*

I was a bad, bad boy
Looking back at a time and an act

The deliberate chipping of rock is a climbing heresy — and I've done it. I began climbing as a skinny disenchanted teenager in Boise, Idaho. My peers, though not so physically meager, were equally disillusioned. We were spoiled products of the middle class who found its values short on substance. Climbing fit the nihilist credo of our generation — a meaningless pursuit in a meaningless world. Rejecting the established order, we created our own social criteria. The ability to ascend area boulders became a hierarchical yardstick.

The best local boulders were castoffs from the abandoned Table Rock Quarry. The sandstone chunks had been blasted from their moor-ings by turn-of-the-century State Penitentiary inmates. The rock varied from banded and pebbly gray to perfectly cleaved fine-grain gold. Our sessions found us pinching drill scars, smear-ing blast marks, and pimping off the rough and regular dentition that edged the better blocks.

One classic boulder problem was on Red Rock, a rectangular cinnamon-gold plaque in the heart of the quarry. In our pecking order, a successful ascent promoted one from total loser-dom to membership in the elite upper caste of rejects. Dubbed *Spidermonkey*, the problem was essentially a set of fat edges on a 17-foot-high, 85-degree wall. The edges led to a layback jug, then a long reef to the summit. Our outstretched limbs and crunched-up feet at the crux inspired the name. Such moves today would hardly rate V0+.

It was our first year of climbing. I was competitive. I had to be. Out of the dozen in our cast of misfits, I ran neck and neck with another kid for unofficial last place. As a climber I sucked. Ignominy and humiliation were my staple diet. Everyone had done *Spidermonkey* except for myself and that other last-place contender, Dave. We were both short, slight, and untalented.

One crisp fall day, in a surge of angst-ridden blindness, I got the layaway, bumped my feet up, and cast for the incut topout. Then the drama began, because I couldn't kip and wiggle my 98-pound frame up a single chin-up.

I still remember trying to bench press the bar in the dreaded basement weight room of our high school. I struggled — legs kicking like a frog, back arching like a bow — in vain until the coach, a big guy even for a coach, eventually took pity. He raised my burden with one hand, then clanged the bar back to its brackets. Watching him stalk off to the squat rack, I caught the barely discernible shake of his head.

The summit mantel on Red Rock was a defining moment. Both hands were oozing open while my EBs pedaled so fast you could smell melting rubber. Fear and ambition coalesced into a single white-hot impulse. A double-knee scum on the slab led to a final patella-mangling rockover. It was finished. My knees would never be the same. I tottered off the back of the rock, proud and happy, having secured the coveted second-to-last position.

Stepping to the dirt, I envisioned my P.E. coach. Once again he was shaking his head. But this time there was a faint smile on his face — a reaffirmation, however slight, of faith in mankind.

Empires rise and fall. Man triumphs and then, lacking the vision or aptitude to go any higher, descends back into the depths of his own murky nature. And so it was with me that fall. I should have done the ascent and been happy. But I decided to chip the holds off the slab. My intent was twofold. First, I was going to make the problem harder. I figured the thing was quarried with chisels and dynamite anyway. Why not breathe some new life into a worn-out slab? Second, my dark and willful side reasoned that, if I chopped the holds off, my main competition would never succeed on the problem. I would thereby ensure my current standing under the righteous guise of crafting a new challenge.

I did it with a claw hammer copped from my father's garage. This, I told myself, was my gift to the Boise climbing community.

After the hold chopping, I was ostracized. A pall of shame hung over me even when I meandered outside the former comfort zone of my climbing circle. A generation of beginning climbers were deprived of a challenge. Since Red Rock's large edges had also been part of a moderate traverse, I had incurred twice the intended damage. To make amends, I offered to carve the white scars back to a semblance of their former dimensions.

"C'mon," I implored. "I can even make 'em better than they were before!" My listeners were appalled. To ice the cake, Dave climbed *Spidermonkey*. He had been close to getting it before the incident and was undeterred by the disappearance of the major grips. Without the jugs, however, I couldn't climb the problem for two long months. A despairing inertia replaced my hard-earned momentum. Dave reveled in his power and glory.

Time heals all wounds, leaving only scars. History deals out justice with a fickle sleight of hand. Seventeen years later I revisited the quarry. I walked its paths with tender nostalgia and the creeping unease of a criminal returning to the scene of his crime. Most of the futuristic lines had been climbed, several drilled into submission with bolts and pockets. Between the chiseling, graffiti, broken glass, and machinery, the old quarry seemed like a post-apocalyptic choss pile. The old routes, smaller than I remembered, were more surreal than appealing.

The quarry had been reactivated in the mid-1980s and the new owners dramatically blasted away the toprope cliffs at one end. Many of the boulders had been carted away, parceled out for building. I looked for Red Rock. Part of me wanted to touch the slab, a direct and tactile link with the past. The proud monolith was gone. It had been dragged off years before.

I wonder where it went. Chances are it was cleaved into flag-stones for the recent construction boom. Rows of homes now line the foothills, encroaching on what used to be our climbing area. The dwellings of the captains of Boise's burgeoning high-tech industry are trimmed with pillars and patios of gold and red sandstone, the panels slatted and cemented with jigsaw uniformity. They accent trophy homes like gilt-edged frames.

Driving out from Table Rock, I cruised through a new subdivision. The homes flickered past with tedious regularity. Perhaps a chunk of my youth flitted by, now part of someone else's legacy.

First published in Climbing *No. 188, September 1999.*

The Strain

Deciphering Canada's nebulous Andromeda Strain

It's coming down. The rain, that is. Dave Sheldon and I slouch in the rough log sanctuary that serves dual roles as a cooking hut and informal meeting place for campers. Seen through fogged panes, the Icefields Parkway cuts a ribbon of slick asphalt through the Sunwapta River Valley. Beyond its banks, drab humps shoulder up rapidly, only to disappear in thick ashen clouds. The atmosphere is dense with moisture. Buried high in the deepest heart of gray cloud and hidden from view is our goal: Mount Andromeda. The rain increases in tempo. Gray drizzle slowly turns to white snow, then back to rain.

We had arrived in Alberta two weeks ago. Straightaway, we tried to do the striated gothic buttress of the Greenwood-Jones route on the North Face of Temple. There, under the massive architecture of the Canadian Rockies, I witnessed my first serac fall and spontaneous rockfall. During the long night we dozed fitfully on the moraine a safe distance from the base, the vast silence was randomly split as roaring boxcars of ice crashed to the initial talus slope a quarter mile away.

The gloom of a storm front delayed the dawn, but eventually we could see that the upper headwall of our route was coated with ice. We decided before reaching the talus to bail. Five minutes later, a truckload of rubble flushed our intended approach couloir.

Sobered, we turned tail and headed north where, under clear blue skies, we climbed *The Shooting Gallery* (IV 5.9) on Mount Andromeda. Our first Canadian alpine climb. That was 12 days ago.

The two outings were primers for our real goal, the *Andromeda Strain* (V 5.9 A2), also on Mount Andromeda. Our first attempt eight days ago began with a jittery 2 a.m. start from our bivy on the moraine below the North East Face. We woke to clouds and drizzle, and at 500 feet were stopped below the rockband crux by huge mashed-potato sloughs sliding from the upper couloir. Three hours of rapping landed us back on the glacier, soaked and beat. The storm that stopped us was the first in a series of disturbances that would last 10 days. Now we sit in camp, counting off moments to the rhythmic patter.

The *Andromeda Strain* follows a 2000-foot gash bisecting the Northeast Face of Mount Andromeda. A steep 300-foot rock band bars the couloir at mid-height. From there to the upper ice chute is the main crux. The upper couloir terminates in a vertical mixed and water-ice pitch — another crux — followed by the exit snowfields and summit.

The *Andromeda Strain* was first climbed over two April days in 1983 by the formidable Canadian team of Barry Blanchard, Dave Cheesmond, and Tim Friesen. *The Strain,* as it is commonly called, is described by Sean Dougherty in his *Selected Alpine Climbs in the Canadian Rockies*: "One of the Rockies' 'grand cours' routes, it took six years of numerous attempts before it was eventually climbed. It is now one of the most popular of the hard routes in the Rockies."

The British climbing journal *High,* in an account of German alpinist Frank Jourdan's 1994 solo ascent, wrote, "Arguably one of the most difficult mixed climbs in the Rockies ... hard ice climbing with sections of delicate moves on 2-3 centimeters thick and often rotten water ice (70 — 90 degree : WI 4) interspersed with rock pitches up to 5.9 and A2 ... a serious outing."

I met Dave Sheldon four years ago at The Mountain Shop in Fort Collins. Our first climb together was a November ascent of

Alexander's Chimney in Rocky Mountain National Park. We meshed as a team, climbing testy mixed ground and thin, brittle ice while spindrift showered in wave after wave of tiny diamonds. Together, we'd since done some of the most memorable climbs of my life.

We decided on Canada in September 1997 as a great no-frills trip — exotic climbing without breaking the bank. Partners are everything. I'd been up to the Great White North once before on an ice-climbing trip with someone who drove me crazy by the time I left. I'd rather have fun and climb nothing than have a bad time and climb everything.

Here in our shelter, Dave hunches over the stove. It hisses and sputters, occasionally belching an orange ball of flame that licks the slick black belly of the fry pan. A spiral knot of greasy blond hair falls over Dave's eyes. He flicks it behind a dirty ear. Dave's shoulder-length hair is his only extraordinary feature. Usually tied back in a rude knot, it can explode into 1980s glam-rock proportions after aggressive brushing. Otherwise, Dave, age 27, is a middle-of-the-road kind of guy, size medium in everything, quiet, never drinks in excess, likes old Bob Dylan.

He pokes at the contents of the pan with speculative, surgical precision. The brown goo rises in a bubble, pops, and expels a fierce jet of steam. Glop is his perpetually bland combination of basic food groups. Glop drives me insane. I eat it because he always does the cooking. I wonder if it's his way of dealing with the interminable boredom of waiting while the weather decides to change.

We silo the glop. Then Dave makes a fried-egg sandwich.

"This weather is killing me," I mutter.

Dave takes a bite of the sandwich. His eyes never leave the table top. "Yeah," he says.

"I could use a beer," I say.

"Yeah."

"How about you?" I ask.

"I deal with the strain by eating," he replies. "You deal with it by drinking."

"Yeah. Whatever," I mumble.

I fidget. Dave placidly munches on another bite of fried-egg sandwich. I feel as if I am watching someone enjoying something a little too much and too personally.

Finally I blurt, "That's great for you. You've got all that food right here. The nearest beer is 30 miles away."

Dave takes another bite and chews thoughtfully. He nods in gentle nonpartisan affirmation. He chews, his mouth never quite closing, eyes fixed on the worn table. I run out into the rain and build a squirrel trap from the fire grate.

Crouched over the blackened lattice of the fireplace grill, I reflect on our Mount Temple failure and our success on *The Shooting Gallery.* These experiences were my first real alpine outings. In the parking lot, Dave taught me crevasse rescue and short roping for glacier travel. Is the *Andromeda Strain* too ambitious? Can we cope if something disastrous happens? I don't know. But there is only one way to find out.

Dave is a good balance. He is prudent where I can be reckless. I am the dreamer, the guy who comes up with the ideas. Dave is the one who injects reality into the dream. Sometimes I resent him. He embodies the personal characteristics I yearn for but will never have. He is solid, consistent, and adheres to a code of ethics, immune to the winds of emotional or circumstantial disaffection. I am an ethical pinball.

I finish the trip wire and chum the trap with peanut butter. It's all in good fun. I would never take the joke as far a friend in Yosemite once did. He trapped local squirrels under a grate and doused them with fluorescent-green spray paint. The rangers caught wind when tourists began sighting strange animals.

Back in the hut, I sit and stare. Most people dream of vacations where they are free to do nothing. The trouble with our vacation is that we can't just call time out when things aren't going our way and stroll out onto a white sand beach. We need to wait.

We also need to do something, even if it is nothing.

My trap is a dismal failure, but by evening I have chopped and dried enough wood to last a week. In the silent darkness of twilight, life in Boulder is a remote dream. I've been living there for six months. Boulder is fast, frantic, full of social options. It's all about Lifestyle. But like this deserted cabin, Boulder is a lonely place. Dave has been busy with wood, too. He has whittled a name from a piece of kindling. He treats the smooth pine letters with margarine. They spell out m-a-r-l-l-e-e, his girlfriend's name.

Three days later we hike up the glacier and glass *The Strain* with our binoculars. The entire face has changed. Thick white snow softens the craggy rock bands. The runnels are clogged. The main couloirs have slid. Jagged lumps of avalanche debris are chunked up at the base like lumps of melting white chocolate. We decide to let the face settle one more day.

The next morning, we hump bivy gear to the glacier and stomp out a flat spot. The jagged moraine, a bony crest of talus one week ago, is now a gentle snow slope. The day is crystal clear, the sun scorching. Two dots appear on the col below. They grow larger, approaching fast. A voice shoots across the glacier from the deep blue shadow of Andromeda.

"The Strain?"

We shout back, "Yeah."

A muffled "Shit" wafts up the slope, barely catching my ears.

Raphael Slawinski and Marcus Norman, both from Calgary, seem very keen. They move with the animated efficiency of experience. They are disappointed that two slack-jawed Yanks wearing matching baseball caps are gunning for the same route. The four of us sit together in uneasy silence on a flat limestone slab. We stare across the glacier at the common goal.

"So how should we haul?" I ask Dave.

He replies, "I don't know. Maybe hand over hand."

Out of the corner of my eye I see the two Canadians start ever so slightly. They exchange a subtle knowing look, half quizzical, half triumphant: The dumb Yanks are going to haul big packs like a couple of gear freaks. Let 'em break trail halfway up then we'll pass 'em after they burn out. Typical mistake.

Darkness comes and the Canadian guys retire to their tent. Dave and I retreat to our tarp. I strip the frame sheet, lid, and accessory patch from my pack. Now it weighs next to nothing. We strip the rack again. We jettison the jumars. The second will follow with the heavier pack, carrying a few liters of water and some food, assisted by rope tension on the tricky bits. Sleeping bags, ensolite pads, and bivy sacks stay on the glacier. If forced to bivy, we will just sit and bask in the cold.

My alarm goes off at 2 a.m. Neither of us wants to get up. I lie still a few minutes pretending I didn't hear it. Dave stirs just enough to let me know he's awake — but not enough to wake me up if I'm still sleeping. It's a stupid game. I start eating espresso beans. We drink tea and tog up for the day. We trudge across the glacier short-roped with Dave in the lead. When it comes to crevasses, Dave likes to go first. It's not that he doesn't trust me. He just takes it as his responsibility. Fine by me.

By 3:30 a.m. we are at the base of the bergschrund. Our yellow headtorches cast jumping shadows over the gash. The schrund has shifted in the last 10 days. Everything looks different. We pick a new line, toeing on a stalagmite of ice and planting our tools on the left side of the shrund. The altered terrain is unnerving. It sucks out any comfort of familiarity. Dave leads over the schrund, then up into the approach couloir. Six inches of light snow covers brittle water ice.

The ice is thin and spotty. Every so often a pick hits rock, rebounding with a dull thunk. Dave's rack is six screws and one titanium Spectre. The rock gear stays with me. Dave runs out 60 meters, placing two or three screws. We then simul-climb until he has one screw left. This last one, backed up with a pounded-in tool, is the belay. By headlamp we eat up the thousand feet to the first rock band — three long pitches. Thick snow shrouds everything. It has a satiny, sugar consistency, not firm enough for solid purchase, but thick enough to impede progress. My calf muscles scream.

The sun is out when we hit our previous high point. The Canadians are two bobbing dots several hundred feet below. They slowly emerge from the blue-gray shadow of the couloir. We re-rack and I get the first block of four pitches.

On our topo, the route traverses up and right, cutting through the rock band for two pitches and jogging back right for two more. Then a flared chimney system, the key to the upper couloir.

Rotten snow coats the first diagonal rope length. I don't place gear. It would be crap. The next pitch meanders through steep ice tongues and short sections of snow-covered rock. Protection is marginal. Crampons and picks teeter on hidden edges. I belay at the base of a good crack that launches up, leading to a snow bulge. The bulge arcs to the base of a blank overhanging head-wall, which forces a traverse to the left.

The sun is out in full force. We are briefly bathed in seductive warmth. From far below floats the groan of diesel engines. The morning Snocoaches have begun their tour rides on the Athabasca glacier. The view is better up here.

I jam the hand crack with gloved hands. My monopoints scratch on either side. It's not too bad until I realize that the only gear that would fit is in the belay. The Canadians have caught up to Dave's stance, a tangle of rope and slings. After 30 feet the crack ends. I start hooking through the snow, with no gear at all. I try a pin. It vibrates, seats, and bounces out. I try another.

Finally, I resort to dragging both tools through the snow until they latch, then gingerly tiptoe my points up. Forty quaky feet later I'm at the belay — two 3/8-inch bolts, incongruous in this vast wasteland. My ropes drape down in two weaving Day-Glo threads, attached to nothing on the whole pitch.

Dave up, I rush frantically off left as the Canadians approach. They are in position to pass. Heavy granulated snow sheathes the rock. I clip the ropes through a nest of rusty pins — a sound belay, but I have to skip it. At 60 feet, an overhanging bottomless notch breaks the sloping ledge system. A few tension moves from a tricky blade take me to thin ice found through scraping, brush-ing, and plenty of chromoly Braille. Every so often I swing through snow into a likely-looking spot only to have the pick rebound off rock. The traverse is long. The screws run out. By the time I reach the chimney's base we are simul-climbing.

Dave rounds the corner and removes the last screw. My belay is a pounded-in tool backed with a Spectre. He shrugs and carefully minces over the final 20 feet.

"Whose idea was this?" Dave asks.

"All yours," I laugh.

I'm in vacation mode now, smirking. Dave has assigned himself not only the crux pitch of this rock band but also the famous exit traverse and ice bulge.

Dave swims up a narrowing and steepening ribbon of uncon-solidated snow. After 20 feet the snow ribbon ends in a rude V-slot, plump with ripe, blooming blobs of rotten snow. Chopping reveals dark shattered rock, good by Rockies standards, rotten even by mine. The dislodged mushrooms swoop past and tumble down the approach couloir out of sight. A continual drizzle of ice crystals sweeps over my hood. It's cold.

The climbing gets steeper and more awkward as Dave gets higher. The pitch is rated 5.9 A2. Dougherty, in *Selected Alpine Climbs*, writes: "The infamous ... 5.9 A2, the universal grade that is applied to anything that is hard! ... there is an unwillingness to believe that it is possible to pull off sustained 5.10 in big boots and crampons. Hence, 5.9 has become something of a catch-all grade for routes that seem like 5.9 or harder ... Few local alpinists think they can aid climb harder than A2. Thus the 5.9 A2 grade applied to a mixed alpine climb should be taken to be difficult, to say the least!"

Dave balances in the corner. His left monopoint skitches on small edges past his best piece of gear, a Wired Bliss cam in a rotten pod. His usual on-lead cursing begins. I'm used to it. Dave, the most polite and reserved of men, banks up his anger for those moments when he plays raw rage like a trump card. A string of vile epithets pours from his mouth. One of the Canadians who has joined us at the belay misinterprets this cursing as a sign of imminent collapse. He coaches, "Try the monopoint in the 'biner, eh!" Dave acknowledges the advice with a grunt, but instead fights on to a fixed pin. His red suit slowly disappears around the corner.

The Canadians, in no mood to suffer the barrage of ice and rock we will drop from the upper couloir, decide to split. They quickly rig a rap anchor, and leave us their topo, a laminated sheet complete with clip-in sling. It is a generous gesture and a measure of their character.

I follow Dave's lead. Scraping around a block, I hang and curse, trying to remove the cam that has walked and twisted in the rotten pod. We cannot afford to leave any gear and I've already dropped our only Spectre. It's just like climbing in Vail, except easier; there's less ice and the rock is worse. I claw up the chockstone's underbelly and pull myself over the top. The boulder wedged into the chimney is as comfortable on top as it was tormenting on the bottom. Dave is lounging on its flat top with the mirthful look you see on people after they have completed a bit of unpleasant work. I look up. One more hard pitch will take us to where the angle drops back and the exit chute begins.

I had counted on an easy ride into the upper chute, figuring Dave could stretch it into his pitch. I hadn't thought of rope drag. I pause to re-rack.

Standing on the chockstone, I get that bad feeling. It's not like having indigestion or depression. It is an affliction of the spirit. Anxiety sometimes wells up when the reality of what we are erodes the fragile framework in which we operate. People call that framework sanity. If so, then sanity is a mere delaying action meant to buy time. Most people feel the strain. Most either treat it or deny it. Some indulge in it or use it for motivation. You can dodge punches for a bit, but eventually you catch it full in the face. And grace? Grace is only there for those who can ask from the strength of humility. I came to Canada to face my strain. Now, though I am facing it head on, I get the feeling I'm still running away from something. Maybe it's my broken marriage. Maybe it's my crippled faith. What good will come out of all this running? I cannot hope for much.

I stem the doubly overhanging bombay, place a long blade, and lean out to assess the scene. Our topo lists an initial section of 5.8 followed by a nebulous dotted line. The dots are broken by the occasional "X" denoting a bolt or fixed pin. Passage is barred by huge overhanging blobs of snow. Above is camped a truck-sized mushroom. Beyond and slightly to the left, the bombay corner system, blocked by a mammoth chunk of snow coalescing into ice deeper in the chimney, shoots up for 70 feet before arcing back right into a shallow alcove.

The passage right looks unprotected and sketchy — vertical steps clotted with mushrooms. I opt for the left variation. First, I must clear the rotten truck-sized lump. The snow is like hefty Styrofoam. I slice off chunks like a butcher. The torso-sized slabs whistle through the air, free fall, and explode into the couloir below. Debris from the operation coats my suit, seeping down my neck and sleeves. It melts and absorbs into my underwear.

I glance down. The Canadians have escaped. They aren't in danger from the debris. But it's not them I'm worried about. My pick cracks off a big chunk above. The slab wedges between the wall and my chest, shoving me off balance. I tunnel in an armbar, throw off the slab, and chimney up 10 more feet to where the chunk of snow juts out like a roof. My center of gravity is forced outward as the space between the ice and rock pinches down. I have no room to swing my tools. I can't get a heel-toe jam. I can't do it. I don't want to be here. This section was supposed to be Dave's anyway.

"Fuck this thing," I explode.

Dave sits silently, enduring my tantrum. He's been sitting for almost an hour watching the white missiles streak past his shelter. He must be freezing. He advises, "Relax. Do what you have to do."

Awkwardly retracing my steps, I head for the vertical terrain out right, with no dotted lines, no little x's, and no gear in sight. I begin excavating, half hoping to find nothing. No gear means no progress — just the excuse I need.

Over the phone, Barry Blanchard had recalled the persistence the first ascent took. "Everyone who was anyone had already been up there. John Lauchlin, Rusty Baille, and Urs Kallen, to name a few. I think Jim Elzinga had been up on it five times," he said.

"Dave Cheesmond and I both went up twice with different partners. We wound up playing this funny game. We'd get up high towards the rock band and have to retreat. We took turns yarding each other's rap anchors on the way up, then replacing them on the way down. We finally teamed up, and with Tim [Friesen] did the route. At the time it was one of the harder routes in the Rockies."

Now digging reveals limestone slopers for the crampons and harder snow-ice, the core of the mushroom I'd tunneled through. There is too much coverage to find any fixed gear, much less placements. Blanchard had called this section "a soul-searching bit of climbing." I speculatively scrape at the shield of hardened snow. Half in earnest, I spin in a screw. It's better than nothing. I clip the rope and ease right. I sink another screw — good for body weight. Rope tension leads further right, where more skittering and hooking finds snowed-up edges. The feet balance on whatever the crampons catch on. I drive an angle lengthwise along a shallow groove. An improvised high step in a sling reaches a steeper rock face. Above, the wall curls back 30 feet to a lower-angled, snow-choked groove. A few more dicey moves and I'm back to desperate scrapping. Finally, I see a fixed pin. Several feet higher, another appears. At least we're on route. I tension off a final pin and plant my pick into a soft mass of snow. It holds. Axe mantels send me into the groove. Heavy rope drag mires my steps. With our limited slings, doing the two sections as one would have been impossible. Dave made the right choice.

Thirty feet of runout, chest-deep wallowing ends in the alcove. I've moved as much snow in two hours as did in an entire childhood of snow shoveling.

Dave takes the sharp end into the exit couloir. We use the same pseudo-simul climbing tactic that worked in the lower chute. After two pitches, I look around. It's getting dark. Depth and scale distort, blending complex detailed masses of rock and snow into solid forms, transforming the mundane into the fantastic. Our escape chute narrows between towering ramparts of rock, dark heavy masses in the dusk. I feel the same sense of wonderment I had on my first trip up El Cap. It's the kind of buzz that comes when you pass through the unknown. A few shards of ice tinkle past, then a big chunk of rotten snow. A muffled, "Watch me" wafts down, dragging me back to the here and now. "Watch you," I think. "I can't even see you."

I sit at the belay with my butt against the ice. I've got that bad feeling again. I think of Charisse. One day she just gave up on me. I was in Colorado working. She was in the pressure cooker of med school in Iowa, and I wasn't there for her. We were two independent wills joined together by marriage. Two wills walking as one can achieve the impossible. Two wills walking in different directions fulfill the inevitable.

After 400 feet the couloir abruptly pinches off in a blank mass of steep choss. It is almost dark by the time Dave starts up the exit crux. A difficult traverse leads to the lolling tongue of vertical ice that will deliver us to the exit snowfields. This is the sting in *The Strain's* tail. Luckily for us, the traverse, usually a dicey mixed affair, is all ice. Dave scratches up the pitch by headlamp. The last few hundred feet is bad snow over bad ice.

111

We switch off leads. We both gravitate between catnapping and euphoria. At the beginning of one lead I vow to take us to the top no matter what. Two thirds of the rope is out when I run out of gas. Dave finds me nodding off in the dark.

The cornice crests overhead, a breaking wave of snow that looks about 200 feet high. The menacing lip drools. Dave leads. He disappears over the lip and the rope comes tight. Five minutes later I bellyflop over the cornice. It's only six feet high.

The time is 1 a.m. We've been climbing for 20 hours.

We sit on the summit and wait for light. I put on my bivy gear — an extra hat. Dave sits on the rope. We put our legs into our packs. We beat our arms to stay warm. The night is dark and eternal. I'm doing curls with a small boulder as an outline of bluish gray traces the ragged skyline. Deep violet yields to red, then orange. The sun's pale orb breaks the darkness, delivering us from the cold. The light carries hope of a new day and the promise of a long road home.

First published in Climbing *No. 187, August 1999.*

The Fall
An end to innocence

When she hit the ragged talus the whack was so loud that a climber on rappel 20 yards uphill heard it. My friend had fallen moments earlier, plunging from sight in a sinuous twist. Forty feet below, she reemerged as a rolling bundle. She stalled atop a hump on the steep hillside, in a placid sprawl on her side, a tanned right arm draped over her face like a slumbering child.

Seconds before, Beth had started downclimbing a steep section of loose rock. We had been chatting about work, relationships, and climbing ambitions, thoughts and problems now petty and forgotten. She was in mid-sentence when an edge broke under her hand, shooting her down and out, spinning from sight.

I had met up with Beth Coats a few hours before in the parking lot at Eldorado Canyon. It was one of those fresh spring days on the Front Range. The air held the promise of long daylight hours, and a hint of muted excitement. All things felt possible.

When I arrived, 20 minutes late, Beth was pacing the packed dirt. She had already hit up a few passing climbers just in case I was really behind. This was typical Beth. She possessed a bursting energy packed into her hard 5-foot-5 frame. Beth was an Olympic biathlete and world-class mountain-bike racer. Her life revolved around seasonally tuned motion — skiing, running, cycling, climbing. She had broken the 5.12 barrier the previous fall. Yesterday she had road biked more than a hundred miles, this morning already lifted weights for several hours.

We went to the nearby Bastille buttress and climbed several pitches. After the last, we unroped and began skirting off along a chossy ledge system, a rubbly break that contoured the Bastille's right side above steep hillsides. Beth had been assertive as ever. She had carried us with her enthusiasm, taking over my lead on a pitch after I blew the sequence and lowered off. (She warned me not to get pissy about it.)

She started downclimbing a bulging wall rather than taking the wide traverse ledge. I think that, in her fatigued state, Beth mistook this obscure section for a similar descent scramble a bit further on the cliff. My silence at that moment still bothers me.

I stood and watched as she started down. Then she fell. When she hit the ground, my first attempt at speech stuck in my throat with a strangled croak. I choked out her name twice, the second call wavering like a scream. No response. She lay still, as if waiting for someone to wake her.

I threw off the rope and rack and raced across the ledge. The neighboring climber, a young guy, stood anxiously above, poised on a wide shelf. "I heard that. What's wrong?"

He let me make a short rap on his rope, and then I ran around the red sandstone wall to where Beth lay. As I approached, I had to fight the impulse to turn around and leave. I wanted to erase the whole incident. Finally I knelt, touching her shoulder and calling her name. No response. Her hair was matted with blood. The only sign of life was her hitched and shallow breathing, punctuated by a low toneless moan.

Airway ... breathing ... circulation ... airway ... breathing ... circulation ... I repeated my first-aid mantra over and over. The adrenaline sang in my head, bright white noise. I was a trained EMT-B but I had never worked on real trauma, certainly not on a friend.

Beth's breathing was labored and raspy, desperate-sounding. In addition to the head injury, she looked to have a broken arm and wrist. The lone climber dashed over and helped roll Beth on her back, maintaining crucial spinal alignment. He then sped down the hill to get help at the ranger kiosk.

I held Beth level, with my knee propping up her left shoulder. I did the head-tilt-chin-lift procedure to keep her airway open. Blood from the head injury made my fingers sticky. It was hot in the sun. The air smelled of dirt, sweat, and blood.

What followed were the longest minutes of my life. Beth repeatedly stopped breathing. She trembled, jaw clamping shut like she was fighting some rising menace within her body. I thought she was dying. I tried several times to pry her mouth open to assess her airway, held my ear over her mouth to listen for the next breath before frantically readjusting. I prayed under my breath that God would let her live. I pleaded with her that she was tough, tougher than I could ever be, and that she needed to breathe. I wanted help to arrive to take the responsibility from me.

Two climbers wandered up, then an off-duty medic out for a spring hike appeared, and took over airway management. I ran down the hill to look for the paramedics. Twenty minutes after the accident Beth regained consciousness. She wondered where she was. She cried, wanting to go home. She tried to get up but her legs seemed distant. She kept calling out for her boyfriend.

The search and rescue team took her out half an hour later. Then I cried, releasing the tension and feeling the enormous weight of loss. Alone, I choked out, "This is not worth it. It all isn't worth it."

Nobody was there to validate my revelation. This incident or any like it nullifies the seeming glory of our pursuit. Climbers talk about ethics and what climbing means and what climbing is all about. When Beth was carted away it was as if someone had taken my passion and reduced it to frivolity, a game of petulant children.

Today Beth is paralyzed from the navel down. Her vertebrae were displaced in several places, and she experienced an almost complete transsection of the spinal cord. She suffered broken fingers, a broken right humerus, broken left ulna, and hand. Self-propelled motion had been the focal point of Beth's life; it still is, but now ordinary movement is hard. Plans wisp on the horizon for a return to climbing, maybe a trip up El Capitan. Skiing and hand cycling are potential outlets for Beth's competitive urges. Beth bravely endures daily hurdles and tedious physical therapy. But for now, most of her time and energy are spent managing chronic pain.

Those around her have experienced the ripple effect. For me, a certain innocence is gone. Since the accident I tense up whenever I see someone scrambling unroped or sitting by a cliff edge. I can't stand to watch. Sometimes on a climb I wonder what the point to this activity is when it can cause such grief. Sometimes I am seized by mortal fear in the most unremarkable climbing situations. It is like the impossible happened, a charm broke, lightning struck.

First published in Climbing *No. 187, August 1999.*

Terminal Man
Marvin always took the direct route

In nearly two decades of climbing, I have seen scores of climbers come and go. I remember them sometimes for what they climbed, but mostly for who they were. Some faces have receded into the junk-laden corners of my mind, buried under the detritus of memories. Others linger on, conjuring up an easy smile — happy days, good routes, good people. A few old faces shimmer unpredictably, like apparitions. In certain psychic moments, their masks emerge with the dreadful immediacy of an early-morning dream. At those times I wish they would stay dormant, buried deep. We are haunted by the faces who taught us, sometimes in hard ways. Loss gives us perspectives, for better or for worse, we would not willingly acquire.

When I was 16, about a dozen of us started climbing. Of that number only a few still get out, mainly for the short crag or boulder session. Back then, we climbed at least four times a week in an abandoned quarry above my home in Boise, Idaho. Our band was a fringe group, obsessed and enthralled, well marginalized from others our age. I don't know whether we chose to climb because we liked it or just because we had to be part of a group, any group. Maybe we sensed unanimously that no one else would have us.

The crisp and obtuse quarry walls, graffiti-adorned by weekend partyers, had been blasted into corners and flat planes. These 40-foot walls had to wait — it was several years before we would pick up on the baffling game of chockcraft and rope work. Instead we bouldered on the discarded blocks deemed unworthy by the quarry crew. Sometimes value is where you make it.

I remember one viciously hot summer day at the quarry. The sun tracked across the sky like a glaring white eye. We sought shade like refugees. The problem de jour materialized by default. Veiled from the sun, the start was cool and dappled with diffused light. It was easy to play on the opening moves, a series of grainy slaps extending high into the rarefied red zone — limb-breaker territory. We took it for granted that no one would seriously attempt to grab the lip, much less surmount the teeter-totter top out. The reason was obvious: The drop zone was a chaos of haphazardly scattered sandstone file cabinets, cool air seeping up from the black gaps in between.

In succession, we would shamble up, fake an attempt, and stage an Oscar-winning retreat. As we stepped off the ground, our faces were masked with the facade of budding machismo. Beneath the posturing was fear. We were only going through the motions — that is, except for one of us. A kid named Marvin stepped up to the boulder. He was a thickset guy who made up for a certain lack of grace with raw aggression. As he chalked up, his gaze possessed a disturbing primal quality. Marvin slapped up, sucking his feet in. He crouched, setting up to launch for the lip. His movements were frighteningly deliberate, a stark contrast to our flaccid posing.

Marvin pulled with his left hand, thrusting hard with both feet. His body arced purposefully with an irreversible momentum. His right fingers caught the rounded lip of the summit at full extension. Suddenly the right foot pinged off. He sucked the foot up, over-gripping in terror. Then both legs swung loose.

Marvin stalled for a moment, weightless. Then he plunged down into the jigsaw of angles. We had to drag him away, a mass of cuts and bruises. In his pain, Marvin was nearly ecstatic. True expression comes at a price.

Marvin exuded tension, a palpable undercurrent of violence

and unease. He was about 6 feet, 4 inches tall and 250 pounds, so strong he could lift up one end of his Volkswagen. Driving, he would speed about town, occasionally throwing perfectly executed bootleg turns for fun. Marvin could be gentle, standing up for his friends, defending us from larger opponents. You could always count on him to be there for you. More than once I pulled a little harder on scary problems after a reassuring glance down at Marvin. It was of great comfort to see his massive form spotting me, hands raised, blue eyes concerned and attentive.

He was also goofy, like a little kid. During one bouldering session, he made the same annoying, high-pitched "eeeeeeiiiiii" noise for hours on end while tickling the crown of everyone's head. We couldn't get any hard problems done that day because he kept us laughing, unable to hold even the biggest jugs. You could tell him to stop. But you couldn't make him.

One Saturday night, dragging Main Street in downtown Boise, a guy in the right lane flipped Marvin off at a stoplight. The pretext was a real or imagined lane encroachment. The conflict escalated as the two cars halted in adjoining lanes and exchanged curses. Marvin's antagonist sneered, hurled a final insult, and turned to face the traffic light, which was about to turn green. He rolled up his window and passed a joke to his companion. He thought himself immune from attack behind a pane of safety glass. The light turned. Marvin's fist struck the side window. His knuckles burst the glass and his arm sailed to full extension, shattering the man's jaw. Traffic stalled at the stoplight, halting the winking glitter of weekend cruisers. Marvin gunned off in his Volkswagen. Chevys and Trans Ams were soon barreling past a stationary Firebird, whose driver was slumped over the wheel — out cold.

My best friend and climbing partner at the time, Cade Lloyd, first introduced Marvin to roped climbing. To demonstrate fifth-class technique, Cade led and then toproped a crusty 5.7 crack at one of the local crags. He belayed Marvin, who found the route difficult yet doable. Then, out of boredom, Cade soloed the climb. Marvin watched intently from the ground. He then also wanted to solo it. An argument ensued and Cade finally managed to convince Marvin to let it be. The next day a sly Marvin returned alone. A slight morning drizzle had glazed the stone with patchy dark moisture. He fell at the crux near the top, thumping the ground and rolling an extra 50 feet to the road. He broke his hip, one leg, and an arm. A lesser man would have died.

Some of us who first touched rock in Boise stayed in town after high school. Some left to college, others migrated to exotic cliffs in far-off states like California and Arizona. I went to college in northern Idaho. One day I picked up a paper and read that a guy named Marvin had been shot to death by a state trooper.

Apparently, he had stolen some gas at a service station and led the police on a high-speed chase. He was run off the road and came out of his car shooting. The highway patrolman had no option but to return fire — he had a neat round bullet hole in his Smoky Bear hat to prove it. Reading the report, I was shocked yet not surprised. To this day Marvin's memory disturbs me, though I am glad I knew him. Sometimes we cross paths with such rare and terrible events.

I can't say Marvin's time on this earth was essentially different than any of our own lives. He lived out who he was just like the rest of us do every day. His actions were more abrupt, the line he chose more direct. In a sense, he was more honest than most: he did not fabricate the mental structures necessary to avoid life's essential question. Maybe he'd explored and abandoned them, found them lacking in structural integrity. Marvin was ill-equipped for modern-day escapist meandering. An unanswered yearning welled close to the surface of his soul.

Marvin showed me the redeeming qualities to be found in all humans, even the dispossessed. I just liked the guy. When you weren't intimidated, he was really funny. I see a lot of myself in fringe people — I fight and question the issues of life in the same way — but for some reason my way is less obtrusive. Perhaps it is just cowardice.

I picture Marvin's end like I remember him climbing — moving with his entire being — regardless of consequence.

First published in Climbing *No. 183, March 1999.*

Partners
I don't know why I kept climbing with Cade

Cade Lloyd was my first climbing partner. We started out bouldering together as friends in high school. Over the next decade we shared countless climbs, ranging from crusty topropes to Grade V and VI walls in Yosemite. I learned a lot from Cade — mainly lessons in humility.

Cade was a solid guy of few words, good with his fists. He always climbed better than I did. He was bolder and stronger, and had better natural technique. From the start, I bumbled in his wake. In our daily bouldering sessions, Cade would rib me. I gave him plenty of opportunity. More than once, I'd dismiss a boulder problem with a wave of the hand. "Looks easy ..." After my ensuing slapstick failure and plunge, he'd always be there to give a hand and brush me off. Then he'd say, "C'mon, Petey. Looks easy, remember."

In our shared passion, bouldering, Cade's edge was often huge. In the middle of the local quarry rested a boulder called Mountain Home after words scribbled in colorful graffiti on its front side. The jutting prow of Mountain Home's east end held a slappy problem that started with a jump to a sloping mantelshelf. Cade ticked it in a few tries and soon had it wired — a quick hop and smooth pull into a palm press. I, however, failed for a year before finally sticking the opening jump. The only trouble was that I found it impossible to wiggle over the lip. Knee scums, belly flops, and desperate palm slapping were to no avail. Another year passed before I succeeded with a crude sternum-grating pop for a higher sloper. I was psyched: I'd never have to do it again.

Cade also burned me off on roped climbs. The Quarry had a classic 5.9-plus called *The Burning Bush* — my ultimate goal. If I could do *The Burning Bush,* I'd be finished with this momentary diversion of climbing and would get back to a normal life.

Cade toproped it first. He had the gunnery and headset to master the intricacies of jamming and laybacking. I was reduced to a flailing mess of skinned elbows and knees when I finally followed suit.

A few months later, Cade led it, boldly running the rope out on nuts in sandstone. A few weeks later I led it after extensive rehearsal.

Then Cade declared that he was going to solo it. I told him he was crazy. I was laughing, but on the inside worried he might be serious. He was.

Several days later as I cowered under the incut base — too scared to watch — Cade powered up *The Burning Bush* with nothing but an old elbow-dipper chalk bag.

That night we celebrated with cheap swill vodka. I tried to get him back by mixing his drinks so strong he ended up laid out like a jellyfish on our friend's parents' front lawn. Even in sodden unconsciousness, Cade mocked me. He sprawled in the cool grass with a contented grin on his face, arms at full extension, feet kipped parallel with his hands. He looked like he was climbing the crux in his sleep. We dragged him out of sight into the bushes.

Like many good friends, Cade and I argued. Sometimes we wouldn't talk to each other for weeks on end because we'd be proving something, supposedly to the other. One day, we stormed into an argument about the utility of hand jamming — though we'd never come across a true hand crack in our lives — and both crossed the lines of respect. A week of mutual blacklisting melted into the kind of understanding that only friends can claim. We went climbing, he let me burn him off, and we never spoke about it again.

After high school we both lingered in Boise, uncertain of the future except that we'd have to leave. Cade made the break first. He entered the Marines. After an early discharge he made a brief return to town and then split on an endless road trip. I remember his last night before leaving. Cade shaved his head in a ridiculous choppy Mohawk, then jumped in his red '72 Subaru, packed with all his possessions. He drove down through the wastelands of Nevada to Joshua Tree. He left behind a concerned family and a loving woman who wouldn't wait forever for this bit of masculine self-actualization. She was a smart woman.

Cade ended up in Yosemite working for the Curry Company. I followed suit, but as usual it took me a long time to match such a bold move. In part spurred on by Cade's intermittent postcards telling of the rock that had filled our early dreams, I dropped out of college two years later. Seeking nothing but climbing, I moved to California, eventually finding myself among the dispossessed of Yosemite.

It was a reunion for Cade and me. One of the first routes we climbed together was the Cookie Cliff classic *Outer Limits*. During the interim, I had climbed plenty of hard cracks elsewhere. This was my chance to prove how much better — better even than Cade — I'd gotten.

"Looks easy," I said to Cade. "It's only .10a, right?" Cade nodded with an old and knowing smile. He nipped up the pitch with fluid precision, placing the occasional piece before reaching the hanging belay. The rope came tight.

"You're on!" drifted down.

"I'll be up in a second," I yelled with devil-may-care flair.

The first section, the technical crux, was easy. A couple of smooth layaways, some edges, and a few jams led to a nice stance. Above lay nothing but a stretch of cruiser crack. My only care was how stylish I would look on it. What I didn't realize was that all of the cracks I had climbed until that point were either finger jobs that lent themselves to face technique or so featured they weren't really crack climbs at all.

After 10 feet of jamming I noticed a strange crampy feeling in my thumb. I began to paw at the lip of the crack, seeking an edge. My feet weren't supporting me, either. They seemed like they were too high or too low. What had looked like a short stretch began to feel endless. I kept going, struggling to look casual. The crack widened.

There were no face holds or creases. I began what I envisioned as an elegant section of laybacking to pass the wide bit. Unfortunately, the edge of the crack was flared and smooth, and I was pumped. After 10 feet I gave up any pretense of composure and began blindly slapping up the left edge, feet skidding. The crack finally pinched down to good hand size. I tried to shift delicately from the layback to the jams — and promptly greased out. Thirty minutes of falling and resting later, I got to the belay. Cade looked at my gasping, pasty face, chalky lips, and bloody hands.

He laughed. "What do you think about the next pitch, Petey? It's only .10b."

Time passed, and we kept climbing, eventually drifting into our own worlds. I adopted our sport as an obsession while Cade treated it as recreation. I've gone on to chase other climbing dreams, some of which are still distant castles. Cade has settled into domestic bliss — easy for him since he always got the girl.

Last month I was at his wedding in Boise, honored to attend and privileged to be the best man. As I stood to Cade's left watching him recite the vows I was struck by an old, familiar feeling. His blushing bride was a woman I had chased while living in Yosemite. For all my efforts, she wanted nothing to do with me. I convinced her to go out with me only one time. It was New Year's Eve, and I got drunk and retched in the bathroom. One day she saw Cade and that was it. Some things never change.

She was a smart woman.

First published in Climbing *No. 190, December 1999.*

Meru or bust
The waiting is the hardest part

Time is the mountain that will break us. We are surrounded by mountains — piles of rock, snow, and ice. They endure. We can't. The best we can do is scratch about their flanks, trying to climb them — often failing, sometimes succeeding. Even the sensation of winning against the odds doesn't last. A summit achieved generates new ambition.

Eric, Dave, and I sit in our tents. The snow patters like a quiet invasion. A rumble shakes the glacier. Another avalanche. Two weeks ago when we were still green, we would have started wide-eyed and jumped to the door. Now, after weeks of storm, we don't care. The rumble subsides. Eric doesn't even have to look up from his book to determine the slide's location. He just states in a monotone, "To the left."

I turn the page of the book I'm reading. Five minutes later another rumble builds. I mark the page, put the book down, and kick the side of the tent. A buildup of snow slithers off the tent fly, sloughing off into an angled heap. I turn onto my side and open the book. The other rumble subsides. "To the right," Eric mumbles. I turn the next page.

It started at 5 a.m. on August 19, 1998. We woke up in Boulder to begin a trip. The night before the three of us — Dave Sheldon, Eric Greene, and I — had packed mounds of gear, food, and hardware into 13 duffels. Dave, 28, is a longtime mountain partner, 5 feet 10 inches tall with long blond hair and a medium build. We've climbed together for years, from winter climbs and big-wall firsts, to alpine climbs in Canada. Dave and I click. This trip is our first chance to try our hand in a bigger range. Eric, 34, is my bro and a rock-climbing partner. He is tall and lanky, with the lungs and legs of a former cycling racer. An aspiring photographer, Eric was invited when another team member dropped out due to finance problems.

Our plan was to climb a peak called Meru Central. Meru, whose name means "the center of the universe," is a mountain group in the Garhwal Himalaya, India. Our goal is the central unclimbed summit of the Meru massif, referred to as the Sharks fin for its dorsal-like profile. The Sharks fin clocks in at around 6500 meters and has been attempted by strong teams from Great Britain, Japan, Austria, and America. In the fall of 1997, I got tired of hearing about everyone else's climbing globetrotting and decided to go overseas to climb something. Meru was suggested to me by Mark Synnott during a climb in the Black Canyon of the Gunnison. Within the week I saw one color picture of the mountain, was sold, and applied for a grant. The peak had a beautiful and savage symmetry. It was dying to be climbed. A grant award from Malden Mills covered the initial cost. Then we started saving.

Now, a year later, we met our fourth partner, Jamie Pierce, at LAX. I'd only met Jamie once, a brief encounter two years prior. His credentials are impeccable. He and Dave were partners from way back. Jamie, 27, is medium height with brown hair and a formidable build. His reputation as a fearless man of action precedes him. A life as a guide and adventure consultant sees him traveling year round to places like French Polynesia and the Antarctic. His derring-do — straight out of a Clive Cussler novel — recently earned him feature coverage in *Outside* magazine. He'd flown in from Seattle, the travel day starting at 2 a.m. He'd been guiding back-to-back trips and the day before found out his stepfather required emergency surgery. The fatigue was written on his face. LAX was hot.

As the plane lifted from Los Angeles, I was glad to be off — no more articles to write, no more expedition paperwork, no more domestic worries. Despite the relief at departure, I couldn't sleep. Jamie and Dave caught up on each others' lives. Eric and I filched beers from the stewardess and giggled like kids.

The cultural transition was inexorable. On the screen, the Wedding Singer lamented in New York English. Eric and I laughed when we heard the jokes. The rest of the passengers, mostly Chinese, laughed a few seconds later when the joke hit the screen in Chinese subtitles. Our flight unpacked in Hong Kong 13 hours later. For everyone but Jamie, this was the first time in Asia. The new Hong Kong airport is a breathtaking gallery of glass and metal — the largest enclosed building in the world. Red stars of the People's Republic of China glint on the collars of machine-gun-armed security guards.

When we boarded our United flight for New Delhi, the upholstery was dingy and reeked of human grease, garlic, and cumin— the smell of Asia. The flight was almost empty, sparsely populated by a few Indian families. We took over rows and stretched out to sleep.

Before dropping off, I wrote in my journal, "I hope the designations of responsibility and leadership work well. We all know each other except for the Jamie-Eric, Dave-Eric, and Jamie-me area. Jamie seems the level sort. He almost charmed an attractive Hong Kong attendant into giving him a first-class seat. I hope the leadership roles evolve as we start the game for real — when we get off the plane ... I only worry a small bit about Eric's reactiveness and dislike for any authority ... there will be no room for quibbles when we are on the mountain. Jamie (an American Alpine Institute guide) knows altitude and mountaineering logistics, Dave has the level head and bullish determination. Eric has the least experience in the mountains, probably more of the wall-type stuff, but ... I see in him a strange gutsiness and rise-to-the-occasion pluck that I've seen in (Jeff) Perrin."

When we landed at the Indira Ghandi International Airport, on August 20, the local time was around 11 p.m. We had been traveling 25 hours. Wheeling our 13 bags to the street, we passed through the door into a paved lot enclosed by a high chain-link fence. The heat and humidity hit us heavy and torpid. Travelers milled about on our side while a brown sea of humanity clutched at the fence. Some held up ratty signs hand-drawn on cardboard. Assailed by offers for rides, we dodged through a general melee, fresh meat for the panhandlers. We met our liaison. Several hours later, the day mercifully ended with a whiskey in our hotel rooms. I was dazed and tired, frazzled.

As the next few days unwound, we acclimated to the noise, pollution, and whirling kaleidoscope that is New Delhi. When you get past the initial impressions, you discover a richness absent in America. Poverty and wealth, ugliness and beauty, education and ignorance exist side by side without the compartmentalization of the west. On a main street we saw a beggar with a deformed lower body and suppurating sores. He dragged himself along with his hands, shoes on them. He stopped to rest in front of a shop that sold leather jackets. A beautiful girl in a stark white robe sidestepped him without expression.

Our agency, Ibex Expeditions, is operated by Mr. Mandip Singh Soin, who guided us adroitly through the maze of paperwork and travel logistics. Though working with an agency might have robbed us of the chance to deeply interact with the culture, we were saved time and energy.

Eric and I did the tourist-shopping thing one afternoon. We hired a pedi-cab — a three-wheeled open metal box powered by a two-stroke motor. The driver, Raj (half of India's male population seem to be named Raj), took us to shops where the owners give him a kickback on sales. A softy, I bought early in the negotiations, while Eric drove such a hard bargain he pissed off the locals.

As we spent time in our new surroundings, the four of us started to connect. To one degree or another, we all got sick, our guts assaulted by legions of unaccustomed microscopic bugs. Diarrhea and gut pains. Eric said it was like " being hungover all the time — without the pleasure of drunkenness." A cycle of Cipro staved off any serious illness. Our new mantra was, "Cipro, Cipro, it should be known as shit-pro."

Our journey to the mountains began with an eight-hour bus ride. We groaned down the middle of traffic moving in four lanes on a two-lane road. Thick smog produced a constant twilight that cut visibility to a quarter mile. We were on a bus with two drivers, our cook, his assistant, our agency liaison, and our Indian Mountaineering Foundation Liaison Officer. The dust, the noise, the endless honking, and smog led to eventual numbness. I fell asleep and woke to a bone-weary deadness. My white T-shirt was brown from the smog when we arrived at the town of Rishikesh. The journey had taken us to the base of the foothills. Distant mountains shimmered in the enervating heat.

At the day's end we staggered off the bus to our hotel. The elevator was broken. It sat at the bottom of its shaft like a broken promise. Eric and I woke up tossing and turning at 3 a.m. A knock on the door and Dave entered. He'd broken the air conditioning in his room. He started fiddling with ours. A few sparks and buzzes later, there was no air conditioning at all. I turned on the TV. A dancing Sikh displayed his magic before a backdrop of demure and modestly clad women. The Hindi voices faded into the latest Smashing Pumpkins video.

Dawn broke calm and gray. Women and school kids entered the street. Bullock carts, bicycles, and lorries began to traffic the narrow road. The sun hit an adjoining tin roof where shirtless men dipped their heads in water.

Another day of travel took us through winding hills and broad green vistas. The land was contoured into tiered flats for growing crops. The wide brown river swirled like chocolate milk as we gained elevation. Monkeys played in the trees. Rishikesh marks the start of a pilgrim road, whose path we would follow. The journey is made by devout Hindus who wish to trace India's sacred river, the Mother Ganga or, Ganges, to her headwaters. The source of the Ganges lie in three major tributaries. Our road followed the western tributary, the Bagarathi river, to its source high in the Himalaya. We were getting high enough to feel the cool of the mountains. It was like waking up from a heavy nap. I could finally think.

The roads were whimsical tracings. Deep gorges, towering crags, and temples all perched improbably over violent rapids. My view from the right side of the bus was frightening. The wheels churned inches from the edge of a terminal drop shot straight to the river. A wreck would be hugely fatal.

The monsoon rains had tapered yet not abated. Flooding and mudslides washed out sections of road. By our second day out of Delhi we were mired in a mudslide. Toward dusk, our bus tried to negotiate the soupy mass of brown slurry. After hours of digging we backed out, ferried loads, transferred to Jeeps, and got involved in an abortive dash through the bad parts of the road. We reached a cul de sac near midnight. A mass of boulders and gravelly mud had just wiped out the road. It would take dynamite to open a breach.

An extra day saw us to the trailhead — the village of Gangotri. On the way, Jamie, a forthright man who has been known to deliver preemptive knockout blows, nearly punched our Jeep driver. It's a point of honor among local taxi drivers to demonstrate reckless abandon behind the wheel. To compound things, the driver was smoking charash, or handmade hashish rendered from plentiful wild marijuana. Jamie, who'd had an acquaintance killed a year before in just such a situation, rebuked the driver. We barreled around yet another blind corner. The driver grinned and puffed harder. I begged Jamie not to hit him.

When we reached the village of Gangotri we were in the mountains at last, the sky clear and blue. Streaked gold granite plunged from valley walls that bracketed the town. Gangotri was a powerful, vibrant place bustling with pilgrims and sahdus, or holy men.

In Gangotri the Bagarathi river roared through gorge you could spit across. Our guest house overlooked this frothing marvel. On the porch, we split the loads into 25 to 50 pound units. The porters — a tough-looking bunch from Nepal who work the off season in India — ambled off, some toting 100-pound loads. One was a kid who looked about 12. He stopped and lit up a bidi, or Indian leaf cigarette. I passed the kid a handful of lemon drops. Before eating one he shared them out with the other porters. Our cook was Bam Bahadur. Together with his assistant, Raju, he whipped up the first of several weeks' worth of excellent meals. We started with chicken stock thickened with rice water and carried on to fried rice with spiced peppers, curried beef, dhal bat (spicy lentils), and chappaties (dense bread). Jamie, who studied to be a chef in Chicago, was impressed. Later in the trip, Bam presented us with restaurant quality crepes at basecamp. For now, our meal was capped with creamy custard sprinkled with chopped local apples and the ever present heavily spiced Indian milk tea, or chai.

A days hike out of Gangotri we passed the Gaumukh, or cow's mouth. From this huge opening at the base of the Gangotri glacier issues the Bagarathi river. The water rushed from the blue ice cavern, spidered with faults. For many pilgrims, this was the end of the line, the apex of their long journey from the hot plains. At 12,000 feet of elevation, this is the source of Ganges. Those who bathe in these waters are said to be cleansed of sin. None of us, sinful or not, braved the frigid waters.

The following day we crested a tall moraine where flat expanse of meadow dotted with granite boulder fanned out for a half mile. I passed a group of our porters squatted in the grass throwing dice, smoking bidis, and gesticulating with animated fervor. They were redistributing their newly earned wages. Ahead was our camp, a meadow called Tapovan. Its elevation was around 14,400 feet. Nestled into low turfed hillsides and chinked between boulders were rough dwellings of rock, mortar, and tin. Here the babas, holy men who summer in the meadow, lived. Their dwellings were festooned with snapping lines of yellow, blue, and red prayer flags. Our camp lay at the base of another huge several hundred feet high marking the terminus of the glacier responsible for sculpting the Meru's east face and the west face of Meru's 21,500 foot neighbor, Shivling. Our goal, the central summit of Meru lined up in a gunsight notch formed by surrounding slopes. Above our tents towered Shivling's east ridge, first climbed by Doug Scott, Georges Bettembourg, Greg Child, and Rick White in 1981. They bagged a stunner. The view west was dominated by the Bagarathis, which shimmer like snow-capped saw teeth in the afternoon sun. The air was fresh and cool. Wildflowers were blooming. It was paradise.

We spent the next few days sorting gear and basking in sunshine. Our gradual progress to this elevation had kept us healthy save some nagging headaches. The bouldering was as good as anything in Yosemite's Camp 4. We were soon huffing and puffing up the best blocks in the meadow, a stone's throw from our tents. Back at the main mess tent, we traded stories. Jamie told us of his new girlfriend, Tami, a doctor. He showed us pictures of them in French Polynesia.

He joked, "I think I am going to give it all up after the next expedition. I'll get a fixer-upper house in Seattle, remodel it and become a house husband." Eric pondered his life back in Boulder. He missed his wife, Colleen, and their "kids," a pair of huskies. Dave said nothing. I knew he'd just broken up with his girlfriend of two years, Marilee. The news came out of the blue and shocked everyone. If Dave grieved, he hid it well. He merely nodded in affirmation and politely chuckled at jokes. As for myself, age 34, I'd filed for divorce a week prior to our departure. To suffer divorce is to suffer a death. The last conversation between myself and my wife had marked the end of all our tears, regrets, and recriminations. Of that final conversation, I had written, "Charisse wished me a bad time in India — I think I'll have it."

On August 30 we began to carry loads to advance basecamp. Our path took us through the towering moraine and snaked up the eastern edge of the Meru Bamak, or Meru Glacier. My mind reeled at the scale of everything, from the mountains to the glaciers. Our hike took us to a bend near the head of the Meru Bamak, where we dropped our loads. On this first run our packs were laden with ropes and hardware. Our proposed line, now laid out before us in living color, was to ascend a long ice face to an exposed rib, where we would traverse a sloping ledge leftward to a large overhanging corner. The corner led to cracks leading up the southern edge of the shark fin. Then the top. The climb would cover two El worth of technical rock. In anticipation we'd brought thousands of feet of rope, mounds of pitons, carabiners, and other hardware. We'd agreed to try the Sharks fin capsule-style, with one pair leading and fixing, the other pair hauling baggage. The drag would be getting the gear up the initial ice face — it had to be several thousand feet high and was perched at the perfect angle to avalanche in a storm.

We were getting sorted out as a team and various opinions emerged now that we'd had a good look at the climb. On August 31 I wrote: "Jamie reported some rockfall. The ice face looks nearly as big or bigger than the rock climb ...This morning Jamie especially expressed apprehension and a clear statement that if he doesn't feel right about it, then he will not go. I absolutely respect his judgment ... Eric — doing well (better than most of us at load hauling) with the same caustic humor, furrowed brow, and underlying sensitivity. Dave is Dave. He has been dubbed (because of his prodigious spud consumption), the "potato man" by Bam. He plugs along — seems quite fit and talks only of hows and not ifs. His main statement is, 'we get up the ice face with our stuff — then we look at that spot as being on the ground mentally.'"

Eric was impatient. He wrote: "September 1. I feel good and I am anxious to get on with it, get it over with in a way ... September 2. More resting and insanity! Going to ABC tomorrow. Get on with it already."

Eric's impatience was noticed by everyone. Dave wrote on September 28: "As usual, eating is the big enjoyment of the day. At lunch Eric announced that he was going cragging. All the sitting around was 'killing him.' If that is true he is in for some tough times at basecamp."

On September 3 the four of us headed up to ABC. The weather was stunning, crystal blue skies, no wind, and no clouds. We decided on setting camp toward the base of Shivling with a direct and open view of Meru. Against the choices of the others, I insisted we set up a rude platform on the glacier itself rather than pitching the ABC tents on the talus above. We slaved for three hours rolling boulders and cobbling together a lattice of flat shards. These assumed a roughly flat surface. Jamie and Dave huddled over their eight-foot patch while Eric and I trundled rocks across ours. Everyone worked in silent harmony.

We pitched two tents and busied ourselves with settling in. The air was hot and thin. A dull thud echoed down the hillside below Shivling. Some rolling shapes caught my eye. A half dozen rocks, some the size of refrigerators, had torn from their moorings and blundered down the hill smashing everything in their path. Dust spurted as they demolished obstacles, the shock reaching our ears a split second after impact. We watched hypnotized by the slow-motion progress. The boulders tracked toward us in a beeline. I yelled, "Oh. shit!"

Jamie yelled, "Whoa!"

We dropped our work, turned, and sprinted for shelter among the jagged rocks studding the glacier. Adrenaline and thin air generated a dreamlike slow motion.

Eric yelled, "Get some. Get some!"

We stumbled at full speed, barely covering 10 yards as the crash approached, cowering behind whatever meager shelter we found. The rocks came to a smashing halt a short distance uphill. The rockfall had demolished the site we had contemplated for camp. We were all gasping in the thin air.

"Welcome to the Himalaya," Eric said. We had ran off clutching whatever was in our hands. Dave was holding his toothbrush. Jamie had a spatula. My hand still clutched the lump of granite I'd been fixing to a guy line. My knuckles were white.

Another bomb dropped the next morning. At 10:15 a.m. Jamie knocked on our tent and announced that he was leaving. He cited family commitments and domestic concerns. His stepfather's illness, his new love, and fatigue from back-to-back trips had dried up his psyche for the Sharks fin. One last round of handshakes and he was gone, dwindling to a small dot on the glacier. An hour later I found Dave sitting alone on a flat rock, sobbing. We sat side by side and poked the gravel with our boots. Dave's tears weren't so much for the departure of his friend or for how it affected the trip.

"It's just that he made the decision to be with his family and girlfriend so easily," he said.

"Yeah," I reflected. "It says something about what we give up. Being here shows us what we are all about."

"He knows what's important," said Dave.

"Yeah. I guess that makes us fools. Or worse." I said.

Dave and I stood up, walked back to the tents, and began packing our packs.

Emotions stayed heavy at ABC. Jamie's departure and the issues raised weighed on our already overwhelmed senses. Dave mentioned bagging the whole thing. I didn't want to verbalize any decision, but couldn't remember ever having so much doubt and fear of dying or getting hurt or failing.

Despite the mental baggage, Eric, Dave, and I were poised. By September 6 we had cached gear at the base and hoped to start up the ice face. On September 7 we were all back in Basecamp. Headaches and the weather had turned us back. Rain fell. Snow blanketed the peaks. A British Shivling team led by Simon Yates sat at the far end of Tapovan. Beside them camped a German team whose goal was Shivling's East Ridge. They waited also. We headed up to ABC on the 9th. Our intent was stalled by very bad weather. Anticipation and disappointment frayed our nerves. Eric "just wanted to get this thing done and get the hell out of here."

The pressure builds as each attempt is aborted by the weather. We play endless games of hearts, inventing our own terminology and cackling like chickens. The strain is telling. Dave and I are used to waiting and sitting in silence while Eric, the rock climber, complains about the unchangeable. His continual fretting is annoying.

On September 13 after a stormy foray onto the ice face, we bail to Basecamp. It has been a week of storm and heavy snow. The German party was getting set to look for our bodies on the 14th. We are now known as the "crazy Americans" among the growing population of Tapovan. A Spanish team has arrived along with several groups of trekkers. Another German team has its eyes on the Northeast Ridge of Shivling. We start calling our site, "downtown Tapovan" because of all the foot traffic. For the next days we visit the other teams and hike or boulder during breaks in the rain. The mountains above are wrapped in clouds. On the 15th Simon Yates reports that one and a half feet of snow fall at Shivling ABC. The frequent roar of avalanches echo down to Basecamp.

Talk starts of an alternative alpine attempt on the ice face. The alpine line would avoid most of the rock and be quicker than our big-wall line. With time running out if might become our only option by. Around the 20th we will have to start worrying about getting up anything at all. Our LO is due to report back to New Delhi by October 6. Factoring in travel time and climbing logistics leaves us with only two weeks. Every evening the short-wave radio reports the same forecast, "Stormy, with no significant change." Dave remains impassive, while Eric's opinion changes moment by moment. He asks, "Are we still doing the fin? I think we can." An hour later he states, "I just have a feeling that we will do nothing." I try to stay away from speculation. Talking about everything ruins any chance of doing anything. Still my mind turns over possibilities like a kid flipping over stones.

A few more days of bad weather and two issues are coming to a head. By now the lack of time makes an attempt on the original line impossible. We ask for an extension of our trip to the 12th of October. Our LO and the cooks are reluctant to see any extension approved. The request creates a new tension in camp. Dave and I have talked about the issue of Eric's experience level for the alpine route. We have reservations about his patience and his ability to communicate. We agree that we must work as a team. I have every confidence in Eric's ability to climb. However, we lack cohesion — Eric and Dave have never climbed together and they don't seem to be clicking. As two parties of two, our plan would have worked. But when Jamie left, things changed.

Eric is sensitive to the issue and he writes: "I still have a feeling that Dave doesn't want me up there (on the alpine route) with them. If the chance comes, I'll bet that will come up to the surface again. I'm not too sure how I feel about that? I can see his side in a way, but I know I can do what needs to be done up there."

Dave writes: "Eric is becoming a worry. It seems like he is getting ready to bail out on the alpine climb. I hope he does. His experience level worries me."

On September 17 the issue of who will go on the alpine route is settled. Eric decides to check out the regular route on Shivling, the West Ridge. It's a route made relatively straightforward by multiple ropes fixed on the difficult sections. A solo attempt is reasonable. Dave and I will set out on the alpine route on Meru. The issue was forced by the request for an extension. Eric wants to leave as soon as possible. Dave and I want to stay as long as it takes. The decision doesn't come without regrets.

On September 18 the day dawns clear. We pack for another round in ABC. Eric departs for a recon of Shivling. On the 21st he's back empty handed and by the 22nd the weather has turned to heavy snow. Chess, hearts, reading, and building snowmen are interspersed with conversations about religion, mythology, and politics. The mood is getting dark. At one point we sit in a stupor.

The deprivation leads to a bleak interlude. "Just think, guys, we each spent 4000 dollars to go on a winter camping trip," I mutter.

"Yeah, just think. I might lose my marriage over this," Eric says half-jokingly.

"If it's any consolation, I've already lost mine," I respond. I glance at my watch and check the date. "It should be official as of three days ago."

Eric asks a question, now serious. "Will I still have a wife when I get back?"

"You don't want to ask me that," I say.

Dave sits silently a few feet away in his tent.

Outside another rumble builds. I joke, "I hope that's for us. Then we'll get what we deserve." No one laughs.

The 24th of September sees us at the lowest ebb of the trip. The snows now feel wintry. Our return to basecamp finds everything soaked. This caps an already sour mood. I try to keep up a cheery demeanor. I feel that if everyone else is down, I must be up.

Dave writes: "Pete continues to be 'Mr. Happy'. His attitude is, 'It's not over 'til it's over.' The bad weather does not seem to be concerning him yet .... We only have about 10 or so more days .... To come all this way and spend all this money and not really get to try anything would be a bummer."

Eric writes: "It's hard to tell exactly what's up, but it may be that winter is starting early. The shit just won't stop. No matter to me. Really. For me it's past any opportunity to climb."

"Fools are the only folk on the earth who can absolutely count on getting what they deserve." I laugh at this pearl from Stephen King's The Gunfighter. I've learned not to count on anything. I close the book. Tomorrow Dave and I embark on our alpine attempt. We have our gear racked and cached at the base. With any luck we will be up and down in a week — enough time to get back to Delhi and catch our rescheduled flights. We've negotiated for an extra week, a compromise that we, the LO, and the cooks can be happy with.

On September 28, Dave and I wake at 4 a.m. We posthole through a foot and a half of breakable crust. This is it. Every last bit of psyche that hasn't been sucked dry is focused on this attempt. The sky is clear. The air is cold. From a distance, a huge slab avalanche has bisected the ice face. I hope that it has cleared most of the avalanche hazard from the face. At 9 a.m. we reach the gear cache. It's buried under 20 feet of avalanche debris. The snow is concrete. For the first time on the trip I lose it.

"Shit! This is a bunch of shit!" I try digging at the base of a rock. After a half an hour I realize that the rock is just another fallen boulder. I sink into silent resignation. Dave says nothing. We walk back to ABC. We are down to one stove, no helmets, one ice tool apiece, and virtually no hardware. That's it, our trip is over. I feel like crying.

An hour later a group of Liaison Officers appear. They say that one of the German teams has just climbed Shivling's West Ridge. The Germans reported good snow conditions, surprising to us considering our morning's postholing. The West Ridge's Camp 2 lies above us. It is tempting. Black despondency is transformed into a glimmer of hope. In five minutes we decide to pay an extra $1000 for the peak fee.

The next afternoon we pitch a tent at Shivling's Camp 2. The elevation of 18,500 feet — higher than either of us has ever been. As we begin to melt snow, the stove breaks. It is the final insult. With no stove there will be no water, no food, no climbing, and no consolation prize. The O-rings in the valve stem have disintegrated after weeks of heating and cooking with kerosene and cheap Indian unleaded gas. Constant cleaning chewed up the o-rings and I've lost the replacements in the snow of ABC. I try dental floss, duct tape, and PowerBar wrappers, but nothing holds enough pressure to vaporize the gas. I cut an abandoned tin can, hoping to fill it with fuel, light it and hold the pot over it. I yank out the Dermatone leash — string coupled with thin rubber tubing — that holds a lighter around my neck, cut the tube into sections and slide them into the valve grooves. I prime the stove, light it and wait for one minute. A slight hiss emanates as vaporized fuel ignites. For 15 minutes the stove holds a flame. To keep it going I jiggle the valve stem. The flame gutters and dies. For hours we choke on gas fumes as I repeat the procedure slowly milking frigid water from snow. Six hours for four quarts of water. There is no dinner. We eat a piece of cheese and fall asleep.

We wake up at 4 a.m with nothing to look forward to except

abject misery, dehydration, and the fear of coping with an altitude far beyond our experience. Through the blue light of dawn we climb fixed ropes up a long technical ridge and on through the bergschrund. We reach the notch separating Shivling's twin summits and proceed up the final thousand feet of sloping snow. The snow is a dry crust plastered over slabs. At one point the crust thins out, demanding tenuous crab scuttling over a long and fatal drop. We have no rope, no helmets, and one ice tool apiece. We are thirsty and out of water. I pass the difficulty and begin the final plod up the summit ridge. Five steps, breathe. Five steps, breathe. I choose landmarks to pace out the distance. Comic strip animations dance through my head. I reach the summit. Dave is sitting in the snow. He has been waiting for 15 minutes.

"Where's the top," I joke.

"It's about three feet over there." He gestures over his shoulder.

I step past and look in all directions. The peaks are spread in a crisp, vibrant panorama. The Sharks fin beckons unmolested from the west. I ponder the scene for a few seconds. I turn to Dave, "Okay. Let's get the hell out of here."

It's 11:45 a.m. The elevation is 21,450 feet, 4500 feet higher than we've ever been. It's our first Himalayan trip and our first Himalayan summit. I am ecstatic beyond words.

We went to climb a peak called Meru and we all returned as friends. Our dream was the objective. In the end, it wasn't the objective that mattered. What mattered was that we persevered and did what we could.

Previously unpublished.

The cure

Scotland: A clean slate in a timeless place

Squinting against the sting of spindrift, I watched Fred bob and weave up an exposed free-standing ice fang — the crux second pitch of the *Shroud* on Ben Nevis. Fifteen feet above him and 20 feet above our belay, an English climber — the last in a slow party of three — struggled with an old Chouinard screw.

"Look at this man, he is practically shitting himself," said an impatient Fred, flourishing a tool upward.

The English climber's blanched face glanced down sharply, but his retort disappeared in a flash of white terror as his right crampon trembled, then sheared free of the soft white ice with a sad slurping pop. I couldn't resist — I bonked the pillar with the side of my tool just to fire up his brain. The whole mass vibrated. The column had barely touched down. A few tendrils, curled into windblown bangs, anchored the bottom. It was my second day in Scotland and I felt right at home.

In fall of 1998 I'd returned from a Himalayan trip. We froze our butts off and summitted a peak called Shivling, not the peak we wanted but a consolation prize pulled from the clouds. We tasted the big mountains and were changed. I returned to Colorado for a short bit of Indian summer and a flaccid winter.

My apathy and lack of fitness produced a poor showing in both the ESPN Winter X-Games and the Ouray Ice Festival. Despite the vibrant energy at both events, I wasn't into the scene. I wanted to go climbing on some raw jagged edge away from the sparkle of crowds. My invitation to the British Mountaineering Council's Scottish Winter Climbing Meet, held in March, couldn't have come at a better time.

The Scottish climbing legend Dave "Cubby" Cuthbertson had hooked me up with Fred and his buddy Mat in Fort William, in the heart of the highlands. Just seven kilometers from Ben Nevis and an hour from several other winter crags, the town is a perfect staging point for a wide range of climbing. Fit from countless days on Canadian and Scottish ice, the young duo from Quebec were living the vagabond dream, climbing almost every day while dossing in a filthy crowded flat straight out of the dole era — an authentic departure from the star-spangled X-Games. I was punch drunk, jet lagged and sleep-deprived and fighting a mild Scotch-induced hangover. I'd begged for an easy classic for my first day, but the young bucks knew a good thing — the *Shroud* — when they saw it.

"This route seldom forms and tomorrow, maybe — poof," Mat had said, his hands mimicking falling tons. "We must climb it."

The *Shroud* seldom forms completely. It rises through the center of Carn Deargh, a towering eastern spur of the dark stooped mass of Scotland's Ben Nevis, tallest mountain in the British Isles, Scotland is where winter climbing began. "The Ben'" exudes a powerful aura, haunted as it is by the specters of countless dramas played out against her walls for over a century.

I'd sighed — dead tired, outvoted, and admittedly tempted by what the guidebook calls, "Arguably Scotland's finest ice feature." Now, the wide slopes above the fang gave Fred his chance to sprint around and past the other climbers. Mat and I followed simultaneously, jockeying around the English team in a weird stop-action charge. It was a long solo to the summit — a vague flatness shrouded in thick mist and paved with perfect neve. For a moment the clouds parted to reveal the frosted folds of Ben Nevis, rolling like melted wedding cake into patched green and brown hills. Then the white clouds billowed back and we navigated out by compass.

Two days later I wrestled with *Fallout,* a classic hoar-frosted mixed climb in the Cairngorms. The crag, Corrie an Lochain, lies within easy striking distance of the Glenmore Lodge — the site of the BMC meet. I had by now eased into a pattern — climb all day, eat and attend lectures at night. We 70-odd guests and hosts hailed from all over Europe as well as exotic locales like Iran, Kenya, and Singapore. The lodge brimmed with the cozy vibe of time-honored community and tradition — something you seldom feel in American climbing.

On our first morning, Amanda Tarr, the other American Alpine Club delegate, and I sat eating breakfast. With a disturbed smile, Amanda poked at her stewed tomato, red beans, and gray mealy sausage.

"What am I supposed to do with this?" she said.

"Ask them," I replied. Across the hall, the Russians were siloing the British breakfast. One fellow, seeing Amanda's hesitation, glanced our way as if to reprove spoiled children.

Amanda and I were to share a ride to the trailhead with the German super climber Alex Huber and his partner, a Highland climbing star, Graeme Ettle. Huber was late. We sat in the foyer as the mob rapidly dwindled out the door. At 9 a.m., Huber — shorter than I imagined — strolled past us without a word, hitching up his leather pants, and rubbing the sleep from his eyes. Amanda and I shrugged, left Graeme to wait, and split for the crag with Rob Milne, a onetime Coloradan now living in Edinburgh.

Fortunately, the weather was very un-Scottish (cold and clear) and conditions were superb — three to six inches of rime ice plastered the rock. The crux pitch of *Fallout* was a long calf-burning corner etched in hoar. At the base, I was entranced and anxious. Rob encouraged me to take my time.

"Aye, lad," he said with a grin, "no rush. You'll be up there shitting yourself soon enough."

I torqued out a small roof into the upper corner, an ice-filled finger-width job, clearing rime and cleaning out Stopper placements. On top, soaked from spindrift and hoar debris, I reveled in the total absorption of the pitch. This was what I had come for.

We got in late and missed dinner. In the upstairs pub of the lodge, I was collared in mid-toast by Simon Richardson, a leading Scottish winter activist.

He opened, "Do you fancy a new route? — It's on Ben Nevis."

I was so startled, the scotch nearly shot out my nose.

"Oh, yeah," I said without thinking. "It would be an honor ...".

Simon grinned, "Great, we'll meet at quarter of and be off."

I nodded. Then I asked, "Quarter of what?"

"Quarter of four — as in 3:45."

I sighed, swallowing fatigue while gazing wistfully at the fresh pint of McCaffery's on the table. Amanda was off in the corner sipping scotch and chatting with a gaggle of men who appeared never to have seen a woman before. Later she turned heads again, climbing the sustained *Fallout Corner* and soloing the brittle and delicate mixed route *Ritchie's Gully*.

Hoofing the long grind up to Ben Nevis was a bitch. My ankle was killing me — the vestige of a 25-foot fall from the top of an indoor wall onto concrete. (For the next few days everyone I knew, in a twist on my normal mocking nickname, took to calling me "Big Fall Pete.") Miraculously, I didn't shatter my legs. The podiatrist had insisted that I stay in a brace for six weeks. That was three weeks ago.

A few times I sank to my knees into the oatmeal bog. Our route was a direct path up a bulging wall called Observatory Buttress. The mist settled, obscuring the already confused mass of toothy eggshell ice and pale snow plastered over gray rock. Simon verbally traced the route for my benefit, while I nodded politely and remained completely mystified. Luckily, he was eager for battle, leading four pitches through a jumble of indistinct features, with delicate blind swings to single-tooth hooks in frozen turf. The virtual belays added to the alpine feel — one was a pair of equalized slings on two shallow body-weight horns. For such relatively small mountains, the Scottish hills feel big and isolated. The following day, when Rob Milne and I were on *Men in Black*, a new testpiece on the nearby Fiacaill Buttress of Corrie an t-Sneachda, a helicopter dropped in to pick up a climber caught in an avalanche in an adjacent gully. He survived, but the incident underscored the seriousness of the Scottish hills, which see many accidents.

Simon and I finished in the dark, another missed dinner saved by an order of fish and chips at the Fort William take-out. The mountains' accessibility was surreal: one minute you're fighting for the top, three hours later you're fighting a queue at the chip shop.

The next night we gathered in the lecture hall, my turn for a slide show. The Scottish traditionalists had pegged me as a representative of "American-style" bolt-protected mixed climbing. I knew I was on the firing line.

"Why do ye bother wearing crampons on these routes?" I was asked, and blurted the first thing that popped into my head, "Because I'd look stupid kicking the ice with a bare boot." Surrounded by glowering faces, I figured it could have been worse. I could have been showing them my X-Games slides.

I returned home feeling reconnected, switched on. I had slid from under inertia. Sometimes you go to ridiculous lengths to discover something that's been there all along. A month later I was squinting against waves of spindrift in Rocky Mountain National Park, hooking moss, torquing up ice-etched cracks. I looked at my partner and laughed. "I've been all over the world looking for this."

First published in Climbing *No.192, March 2000.*

Lost on El Cap
You play the game, you take your chances

I met her at Yosemite Lodge. I was a busboy and she was a newly minted assistant manager. She was 19, coquettish, fresh, about five feet tall with straight red hair, dark green eyes, and skin like cream. When she smiled, her eyes and nose crinkled like a pixie.

I wanted to go out with her. Of course so did every other single male who worked in the restaurant. Single. Male. Given Yosemite's dearth of women, the latter almost always assumed the former.

For once, my lowly position came in handy. One night, engaged in the mindless routine of clearing plates, filling water glasses, and reciting platitudes, I watched as the restaurant spun towards a meltdown. A record number of hungry tourists clamored at the door. Around 7 p.m. the restaurant hit critical mass. The waiters and waitresses attended to the patchwork of nationalities like sweaty triage medics.

Managing the host station, my angelic supervisor was caught between famished day trippers and overloaded waiters. It was my lucky chance. I stood, water pitcher in hand, purposely gaping at an imaginary spot on the far wall. She stalked over, flushed.

"We need a six top there," she exclaimed, pointing at a table heaped with soiled linen and dirty plates. I stood slack jawed.

She trembled, "Get on it!" I didn't move.

Finally I said, "What's in it for me?"

"You won't get written up," she snapped.

I smiled. Long seconds ticked by.

I asked, "How about dinner?"

"What?" she said. She recovered and asked, "With who?"

It was my turn to flush. "Well, um, with me."

She paused slightly and then smiled: "OK." She turned, floating back to the host stand with sure and measured steps. I was so excited I nearly dropped my water pitcher.

The dining room in the Mountain Room Broiler opened to a view of Yosemite Falls, thundering down from thousands of feet above. The surrounding rock yellowed into gold, then slowly bloomed orange. We ate by the window and the view had nothing on those green eyes.

My 25th birthday was to arrive in several days. It an auspicious and weighty sum of years.

"Are you planning something special for your birthday?" she asked. In my mind, her question oozed with romantic innuendo.

I stammered, "Well, I, um, I don't have any plans." I quickly added, "Maybe if you have the evening off ..."

Suddenly I remembered I'd made plans months before to spend my birthday climbing El Capitan. I had told my buddy John Pinchott we would try *Lurking Fear,* a clean moderate crack system on the burnished walls of El Cap's west buttress. He'd been keen on the route all year. John was made of stern stuff and would scoff at any attempt to postpone, especially for whimsy.

I was in the middle of a big season of wall climbing. I'd cast off the second guessing and paternal recriminations that had echoed so long and loud in my mind. My schedule fit my passion. I could give my all to climbing during the day. Four or five nights a week I'd give whatever was left to my restaurant job. I was living the dream. Yet even dreams get crowded by the murmurs of doubt. Could I keep living for the next climb forever? Could I spend the rest of my days pursuing self-indulgent ascent? Could this new girl carry the prospect of domestic bliss? Where could it lead?

At the table in the restaurant, my predicament choked me.

Climbing suddenly seemed quaint and vaguely dirty.

But the plan was the plan. I had to honor my commitment, so I backed down even before I had a chance to ask. My climbing plans sounded lame, my words flat. I sensed I was losing critical momentum.

The next day hope was restored. At the Lodge, she handed me a package. "Don't open this until your birthday," she instructed me.

"What is it?" I asked.

"It's a surprise, silly," she said.

She smiled that promising smile and floated through the pines.

On May 23, I was jamming and Friending my way up the initial slabs of *Lurking Fear.* John belayed. John, a fellow restaurant employee, was from New Hampshire and had a fatherly, authoritative side. Once, when we ran out of food on *Mescalito,* as John, Jeff Perrin, and I ate a piece of hard candy each for lunch, he admonished us, "Don't chew your candy, suck on it. It will last longer." (Jeff muttered, "Suck on this.")

John broke a rivet on the second pitch. The wall was blank as a slate. We had no cheater stick or rivet kit, so we rapped to the ground and rummaged in the woods until we found a tree branch long enough to stick-clip past the broken stud. We monkeyed around for hours in the hot sun with ascenders, ropes, and dead wood. I kept glancing down through the trees to the meadow. What was she doing? I could be down there gazing into those eyes. Instead I wilted in the heat as John fished a wired Stopper — taped to a bent and unwieldy stick — onto the next rivet head.

Our first day ended low, bivied atop the third pitch. We could have fixed, slept in the Valley, and returned in the morning. I might have snatched a few moments of her company. But that would waste time. According to John, we were behind schedule and needed every minute to make up for the broken-rivet incident. I fell asleep gazing wistfully into the pines below. I lay on a ledge sifting the monochrome gray-on-gray where the forest met the talus. We'd see each other after the climb. She'd said so.

Our second day on *Lurking Fear* was May 24, my 25th. We climbed seven pitches and retired to an angular ledge below an exfoliated slab called The Pillar of Despair. John was in his por-taledge, I was on a pad on the ledge. As the sun set I pulled out my treasure. The parcel consisted of a half pint of Crown Royal and a birthday card. I tipped the whiskey bottle and drank. I opened the card. It read, "Happy Birthday, Pete. I hope you are having a fun, safe trip. I hope you are thinking about me up there." The words went straight to my heart and the whiskey straight to my head.

I blathered to John about how killer this new girl was and how, at this crucial juncture, I was ready to think about life beyond climbing.

John sipped some Crown Royal and smiled quietly.

On the third day we joined the West Buttress route after another pitch. We raced to Thanksgiving Ledge and on to the top. As we plodded across El Cap's bald summit hump, the upper Valley came slowly into view. It was becoming a familiar view — this was my fifth trip up El Cap. The Big Stone, once an object of awestruck fear, had lost its old mystery. The view from her flanks no longer sucked the breath out of me. The proud summit no longer appeased me. Each step of descent brought not only a cumulative fatigue but an odd anticipation. This time, something besides sodden celebration awaited me on the Valley floor.

We hoofed to the meadow, loaded our bags into John's truck, and arrived at the Lodge late. The next morning, as soon as we'd sorted gear in the lot, I straggled into the restaurant office, osten-sibly to check my schedule. My would-be girlfriend wasn't around.

A waitress and busboy stood in the office, though; hands cocked on hips, they shared the latest gossip. I listened in horror. As word stacked on word, my fanciful construct shimmered, then vanished. Around the time I'd reached the third pitch, she'd taken off to the east side of the Sierra with a guy I knew. They'd returned, all smiles, as I approached the Pillar of Despair. By the time I was pulling onto Thanksgiving Ledge, two pitches from the top, they were the Lodge's hot new couple. Everyone knew about it except me. I'd been on El Cap.

In that moment, as I stood in that office, the world dropped away in terminal free fall. I slowly walked to my car. I drove to

El Cap Meadow. The afternoon sun was softening, casting its rays across the cliff, highlighting cracks, ledges, and hidden features. El Cap looked vast — once again mysterious and alluring. I emptied my haul bag in the dirt and began racking gear.

That year I had one of the best climbing seasons of my life, climbing hard sport routes in Oregon, Utah, and Idaho, and cracks in Nevada; doing indoor comps in California; waking up in the Valley, time and again, portaledged in the middle of a vast granite wasteland. Sometimes I catch myself looking back wistfully at that year with its intense and restless abandon. Then I smile when I remember: I couldn't have done it all without her.

First published in Climbing *No. 196, August 2000.*